Mr. & Mrs. Dewey L. Cochran
4627-
Albuq[...] [...]exico
Telep[...] [...]7

January 1954
Calvary Baptist Church
Dr. Lewis A. Myers - teacher
first three chapters.
April 21st - beginning 4th -
chapter -
Rev. J. C. Moore - Pastor -
teaching -

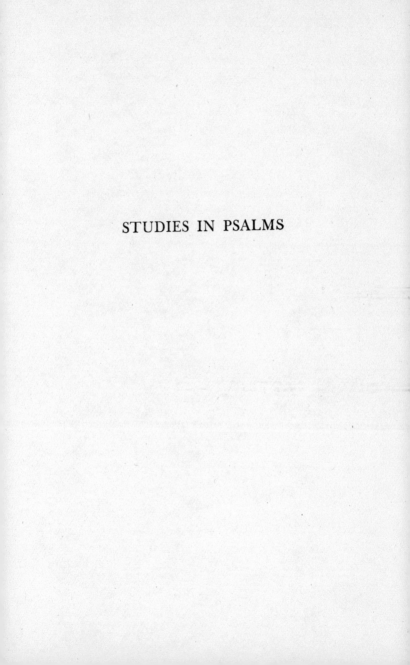

STUDIES IN PSALMS

STUDIES

In

PSALMS

KYLE M. YATES

☆

BROADMAN PRESS
NASHVILLE, TENNESSEE

TO

OUR PREACHER SONS

KYLE YATES, JR.

ROBERT WOODDY

WILLIAM GRAYDON TANNER

The Sunday School Training Course

The Sunday School Training Course prepared by the Sunday School Department of the Baptist Sunday School Board is one of the major means of promoting Sunday school work. Its influence is limited only by its use.

The six sections of the course include studies in Bible, doctrines, evangelism, Sunday school leadership and administration, teaching, age group studies, and special studies. The range of the course is broad, for the field of Sunday school work is broad and requires comprehensive and specific training. Sixteen books are required for the completion of each Diploma.

The study of the training course is not to be limited to the present Sunday school workers. Most churches need twice as many workers as are now enlisted. This need can be supplied by training additional workers now. Members of the Young People's and Adult classes and older Intermediates should be led to study these books, for thereby will their service be assured. Parents will find help as they study what the Sunday school is trying to do.

Special Note to Instructors:

During your teaching of this book will you check with the Sunday school superintendent and see if an accurate record of training for the workers is kept. If not, please urge him to set up such a file with an associate superintendent of training in charge. File cards for this purpose may be ordered at nominal cost from your nearest Baptist Book Store.

J. N. Barnette
Secretary, Sunday School Department
Baptist Sunday School Board

DIRECTIONS FOR THE TEACHING AND STUDY OF THE BOOKS FOR CREDIT

I. DIRECTIONS FOR THE TEACHER

1. Ten class periods of forty-five minutes each, or the equivalent, are required for the completion of a book for credit.

2. The teacher is given, when requested, an award on the book taught.

3. The teacher shall give a written examination covering the subject matter in the textbook. The examination may take the form of assigned work to be done between the class sessions, in the class sessions, or as a final examination.

EXCEPTION: All who attend all of the class sessions; who read the book through by the close of the course; and who, in the judgment of the teacher, do the classwork satisfactorily may be exempted from taking the examination.

4. Either Sunday school or Training Union credit may be had for the study of this book. Application for Sunday school awards should be sent to the state Sunday school department, where forms may be secured on which to make application. These forms should be made in duplicate and both copies sent.

II. DIRECTIONS FOR THE STUDENT *

(*The student must be fifteen years of age or older to receive Sunday School credit.)

1. *In Classwork*

(1) The student must attend at least six of the ten forty-five minute class periods to be entitled to take the class examination.

(2) The student must certify that the textbook has been read. (In rare cases where students may find it impracticable to read the book before the completion of the classwork, the teacher may accept a promise to read the book carefully within the next two weeks.)

(3) The student must take a written examination, making a minimum grade of 70 per cent, or qualify according to *Exception* noted above.

2. *In Individual Study by Correspondence*

Those who for any reason wish to study the book without the guidance of a teacher will use one of the following methods:

(1) Write answers to the questions printed in the book, or

(2) Write a development of the chapter outlines.

In either case the student must read the book through.

Students may find profit in studying the text together, but where awards are requested, individual papers are required.

All written work done by such students on books for Sunday school credit should be sent to the state Sunday school secretary. All of such work done on books for Training Union credit should be sent to the state Training Union secretary.

PREFACE

PRICELESS POEMS are your possessions. Acres of diamonds are near you. Every child in our land has access to these age-old poems that are rich gems available at any moment. Men and women who face frustration and confusion and despair can reach back into this treasure-chest and come out with the answer that is so desperately needed. In days when a vital faith in the eternal God is the most needed treasure, men will find in these poems that which will provide the necessary solution to their problems. Instead of doubt and impatience and despair the seeking soul can find a strange peace of mind, a heart full of joy, and a satisfying serenity that come from recognizing full safety in the presence of the God of our fathers. His heart can be stilled as by a magic wand when the cooling touch of the divine fingers bring their balm of consolation.

These psalmists have provided for us the most fitting language for worship in our day. Every phase of life is pictured. The solution of life's problems is uncovered for us. The Christian discovers the kind of life he would like to lead. He finds that it is possible and desirable to have close fellowship with the eternal God. Step by step he is given the insight into the way a struggling Christian can approach God. With reverence and awe he is encouraged to come boldly to the throne of grace for the solutions and blessings that are available. It is possible for us to combine dignity and fervor in the worship of the One who is pictured for us in the book of Psalms.

We may be sure that no one gets tired of the psalms. They embody the forms of enduring beauty. Their imprint upon the peoples of the earth is unmistakable. They furnish the language for the soul to record its inner longings and yearnings. With moving phrases, with vigor of expression, with color and exceptional vividness, they sound the deeper things of the soul. As one reads these poems he is made to realize that he is following the utterances of a king who is beset by enemies, facing great odds, and walking the way triumphantly. These poems have revealed to us the way men find the living God. When one follows in the path that they have marked, he comes into peace and joy of communion with God.

All down the centuries men have looked to the book of Psalms for the culture of the soul. They have sought to deepen the fellowship with God. Through its pages they have learned to approach him in worship. The penitents have come to God in the words of Psalm 51. The forgiven ones have voiced their joy and thankfulness in Psalm 32. The trusting souls have pillowed their heads in Psalm 23. The grateful ones have poured forth praises in Psalm 103. For model prayers, sincere meditations, happy songs, benedictions, and revelations of confessions, complaint, petition, thanksgiving, and aspiration, we turn to Psalms for the finest models.

I am indebted to the works of Kirkpatrick, Delitzsch, Walker, Morgan, Leslie, James, Scroggie, MacLaren, Sampey, and others who have opened the Scriptures to me. It is impossible to give full credit in each instance for the impression has been made years ago.

When not otherwise indicated, Scripture quotations are either from the King James Version or are the author's own.

My prayer is that this book will help you fall in love with the book of Psalms and become more devoted to our Lord and Christ.

KYLE M. YATES

Houston, Texas

CONTENTS

CHAPTER I
GOD'S HIGH MORAL STANDARD

IF ONE would know the Hebrew conception of a godly man, he will find plenty of material in the book of Psalms. David and those who followed him were able to present striking portraits of the godly man. These poems are brief and colorful. They are as simple as a child would expect them to be. Elemental graces and qualities are described in language that cannot be mistaken.

When Jesus came to fill in the full picture that had to do with behavior and conduct, as well as with the inner motives and attitudes, he already had at his disposal the Hebrew portrait that was ready for his own matchless coloring. We thank God that the saints of old were challenged by the poets and prophets to build into the very warp and woof of their character those qualities that made for the divine approval.

We shall seek in Psalms 1, 15, 24, and 112 to find God's moral standard. We shall look at the man who was approved of God. We shall be strangely moved as we call ourselves to the most simple and elemental duties that make for great living.

I. THE IDEAL SPIRITUAL MAN (PSALM 1)

> *Blessed is the man that walketh not in the counsel of the ungodly, nor standeth in the way of sinners, nor sitteth in the seat of the scornful. But his delight is in the law of the Lord; and in his law doth he meditate day and night. And he shall be like a tree planted by the rivers of water, that bringeth forth his fruit in his season; his leaf also shall not wither; and whatsoever he doeth shall prosper.*
> Psalm 1: 1-3.

In dealing with what has been called the "threshold psalm" we are facing a beautiful poem that could well be the introduction to all the Psalter. In it we are brought face to face with an Old Testament challenge to men on the subject

1

of the blessedness of the life wholly committed to God and the utter destruction that awaits one who leaves God out of consideration. The psalmist believes that fellowship with God is found only when one has majored on learning God's Word, communing with God, and cutting out from his thinking and his behavior those things which are displeasing to God.

This poem describes the ideal man and puts down for us something of his character, his influence, his conduct, and his destiny. Strangely enough these four points are the backbone of the Sermon on the Mount. Jesus was able to find the germ of all of those rich requirements for great living from the bare outline which David gave us.

In this psalm we are treated to the portraits of two men. One of them guards his direction, his leisure, his company, loves and meditates upon the Word of God, and delights to please God in word and thought and deed. The other is the exact opposite, and instead of being secure and fruitful and happy, finds himself completely unattached, lost, blown by the storms of life, and finally destroyed for lack of touch with God. We could hardly imagine a more perfect treatment of this subject that is so close to the heart of the divine pattern.

1. The Picture of the Righteous Man (Psalm 1:3)

In the opening paragraph the righteous man is pictured. Sinners are described in contrast by three words. The first one translated, "ungodly" or "wicked man," is a general term for the person who is out of touch with God. The word *rasha* means literally "unrest." Perhaps we are given to understand that the disharmony which sin has brought into the heart of man has a blighting effect upon the man's touch with God and his heart.

The second word, translated "sinners," describes habitual offenders who have developed the habit of missing the mark or veering from the straight and narrow way and have become established as strays or men who are out of touch with God.

The third word used, translated "scorners," is a word that is well known in the Proverbs. It is their habit to treat with ridicule that which is holy and good and sacred. They are cynical freethinkers with pride and self-sufficient spirits. They are contemptuous in their thought and speech concerning God. Nothing can be done to bring them back to God because they will not only refuse to seek wisdom themselves, but reject reproof in every instance. They are heading for a divine judgment, and no good can come from associating with them.

The psalmist declares that the truly good man, who is worthy of the title, refuses utterly to walk in the atmosphere created by these wicked men. He is unwilling to stop and spend time being influenced by the ones who have missed the aim so tragically. He will refuse to sit in session with the scorners and thus establish himself as one of them.

Thus, we have been introduced to the man who has established these definite refusals in his life. He will not walk, he will not stand, he will not take his seat, in the company of those who are enemies of God. Nothing can induce him to destroy his better self by associating with people who present such a deadly drag on his spiritual life.

Note the threefold form of words, "walk," "stand," "sit"; "counsel," "way," "seat"; "wicked," "sinners," "scorners." These successive steps in the career of evil are religiously avoided by this man who is wise enough to realize that life is too short to be destroyed by such behavior.

When we come to verse 2, we are face to face with the positive principle and the real secret of this good man's life. The torah of the Lord is his rule of conduct. It is interesting to know that that word *torah* is from the verb *yarah*, "to teach," and the one who is interested in becoming a righteous man is tremendously interested in what God has spoken or revealed.

The psalmist tells us that his delight is in the teaching of Jehovah. It has literally become the rule of his life. He sits and enjoys it and meditates upon it day and night. The perfect tenses in verse 1 describe what in all his life he has never allowed himself to do. The imperfects in verse 2 describe what he continually busies himself in doing. He finds peculiar delight in searching and knowing and meditating upon the Scriptures.

If we would know the consequences of his refusals and his delight in God's Word, we will find it in verse 3 which describes the result of such behavior in the life of this godly man. He tells us that he becomes like a strong, sturdy tree that has its roots deep in the subsoil by the water brooks.

That tree, in addition to being beautiful and stately, yields its fruit in its season. The leaves do not fall off. Being firmly planted, it cannot be destroyed by the winds that sweep across the land. Perhaps he is describing a stately palm. We know that the palm loves water. It has foliage that is green all the year round. It is exceedingly stately in growth, and its fruit is valuable.

The psalmist tells us that a life that feeds on God's Word, that delights to do God's will, will find that it is ever fruitful in good works. The combination of clean living, eating the Word of God, and producing fruit, will keep him vigorous inside and out and produce the kind of life that will be a positive influence for good wherever he is found.

He is rooted, steadfast, fixed, anchored, and with such equipment he rides out the storm, unmoved and stronger than ever. His inner self is fed and nourished from an unending fountain of rich treasures. In it all he finds new freshness and growth. His life has access to reservoirs that do not dry up. He is rich in life that abides.

Is this a picture of your own self as you hold this portrait before you and look honestly and frankly into your own life? As you turn the fluoroscope of God's Word upon yourself, what is the verdict? Can you face the storms of life with the assurance that a plentiful supply of riches has been stored up for your own use? Do the roots of your life reach down and tap the life-giving stream that will make for stamina in the hour of testing? God declares that such is his ideal man.

May this study help each one of us to experience more of the stability and fruitfulness of the "rooted" life.

2. The Man Out of Touch with God (Psalm 1:4–6)

When we turn to the other side of the picture, verses 4–6, we see the exact opposite of a tree that is rooted by streams of water. The man who is not in touch with God is like the chaff without root, without fruit, without freshness, without vital inner strength. There is no stability, there is no freshness, there is nothing that will be pleasing.

His character, his conduct, his destiny are all wrong because he has chosen to keep God out of his life. He is now a bit of worthless chaff that is at the same time helpless, wind-driven, insecure, with no hope of permanence or fruit or attractiveness or freshness. Even though his present state may seem to be all that could be despised, he is still to arrive at the doom that is inevitable.

His house is built on the sand. There is no foundation. When he comes to the end of the way, he finds that he has no permanence, no anchor, no rock, no home, no God, no light at eventide. He finds that the way of the ungodly, because he has chosen to leave God out, must needs perish. It merely loses itself in a dark, dark night. It goes out into a trackless, endless, infinite, boundless desert, and while the way of the righteous issues in eternal life, the life of the ungodly is utterly misspent, misdirected, and ends in eternal death.

II. LIKE HIM (PSALM 112)

> Praise ye the Lord. Blessed is the man that feareth the Lord, that delighteth greatly in his commandments. . . . He is gracious, and full of compassion, and righteous. A good man sheweth favour, and lendeth: he will guide his affairs with discretion. Surely he shall not be moved for ever. . . . His heart is fixed, trusting in the Lord. His heart is established, he shall not be afraid.—Psalm 112: 1, 4–8.

This psalm, although not as well known as others, bears remarkable testimony to the blessedness of the man who lives in true relation with Jehovah. It is an echo of the first Psalm, and it describes the condition of the godly man in terms that seem to attribute to the man who fears Jehovah the same qualities that are attributed to Jehovah himself in the previous psalm. He declares that the secret of true satisfaction is the fear of the Lord. This fear leads to a cheerful and thorough obedience to the commands of God. In carrying out the commands of God he becomes like his God. True happiness consists in becoming like him who is at once powerful and gracious.

The character of the godly man is a reflection of the character of God. He is gracious, compassionate, righteous, generous. He delights in making gifts to those who are in need. He stands immovably fast in his resistance of evil and in his faith in the perfect will of God. His conscience is clear and his faith is strong. Therefore his heart is never disconcerted by the announcement of evil tidings, but he remains strong in his confidence because of his trust in the God whom he knows so well and loves so devotedly.

Paul uses verse 9 of this psalm (2 Cor. 9: 9) when he is seeking to encourage Christian brethren to distribute liberally among those who are in need, because giving is an evidence that one is becoming like God, who is love and who delights to give.

The psalmist pictures the righteous man as coming to the end of his way, honored and happy and staunchly anchored so that the wicked look on with impotent rage and finally pass out of the picture from sheer self-destruction, while God's man enjoys the dawning of a new and richer day with all of the glories that heaven affords.

III. God's Requirements (Psalm 15)

Lord, who shall abide in thy tabernacle? Who shall dwell in thy holy hill? He that walketh uprightly, and worketh righteousness, and speaketh the truth in his heart. He that backbiteth not with his tongue, nor doeth evil to his neighbour, nor taketh up a reproach against his neighbour. In whose eyes a vile person is contemned; but he

honoureth them that fear the Lord. He that sweareth
to his own hurt, and changeth not. He that putteth not
out his money to usury, nor taketh reward against the in-
nocent. He that doeth these things shall never be moved.
—Psalm 15: 1–5.

If we would get to the very heart of the psalmist's description of the man who pleases Jehovah, we would come quickly
to the portrait painted in this brief psalm. When the psalmist would show us the exact heart of this man, he first of all
declares that his general deportment is without flaw, that
his activity is right, that his inner thoughts are pure, that his
attitude toward his fellow man is all that could be desired.

It is a big order to seek to know and emulate the full directions given in this psalm. He describes the moral, ethical
and spiritual requirements that a holy God requires for entrance into his select society. For one who seeks to become a
permanent guest in God's presence, certain things must be
met. The psalmist assures us that this remarkable boon is
ours, that we can actually be admitted to the presence of
God, that even as Enoch walked with God, it is possible for
other human beings to have that privilege.

1. Integrity

The question naturally arises, What is expected of one if
he is to enter this holy place and become the walking companion of the eternal God, who is holy and righteous?

The first verse puts the question. The second verse answers
it in general terms. No one is allowed except a man of integrity, a man of justice, a man of truthfulness. Those three
things seem to sum up the requirements. His manner of
walking and acting and speaking is presented. He must have
a walk that is blameless; he must behave according to God's
will for his life; he must be absolutely truthful in everything
he does and says.

The one thing that sums up all other requirements is that
he must have fullhearted devotion to God and complete integrity in all of his dealings with his fellow man. When one

is wholly and completely dedicated to God and desperately in love with him and at the same time right in his attitude toward and his behavior with men, he is able to go a long way toward qualifying as God's man.

2. Justice to God

If one would draw near to God, he must in the fullest sense walk perfectly, work righteousness, and speak truth in his heart. The word "perfectly" is the translation of the word *tamin* which means "sincere, blameless, complete, without blemish." It includes wholehearted devotion to God.

The words "speaking the truth in his heart" would indicate that whatever his mouth speaks, his whole heart instantly goes along with it. He is sincere and behaves always as one who is conscientious and straight in his attitudes and intention. Jesus said, "Blessed are the pure in heart: for they shall see God." It seems that our psalmist has come close to that in his ideal for this worthy walker with God. Before he is admitted to the divine presence for the days ahead, he must submit to a searching examination.

3. Sincerity

Not only are those positive qualities just mentioned to be apparent, but there are certain negative tests that he must face. He is utterly sincere in all his statements. No untruth passes his lips. He avoids the slightest tendency to circulate slander. As God's man he is devoted to the task of protecting his neighbor's reputation. No evil rumor goes beyond his tongue. He is not willing, under any circumstances, to whitewash iniquity or treat a rascal as though he were a respectable citizen. He knows how to estimate men.

A reprobate is one who is not good metal. The psalmist declares that God's man does not treat such a person as good metal and pass him off as the genuine article. It is his right to show keen discernment in his estimate of the character of men. It is not enough for him to despise the reprobate. He must be as strong in his approval of those who are godly and sincere. No matter how insignificant they may be they must be honored if there is in them the kind of basic goodness that will give them standing before God.

4. Personal Behavior

He will be as diligent as can be in the keeping of promises and contracts, even though the promise he has made will cost an enormous sum of money. He must recognize the sacredness and the sanctity of a promise and keep it at any cost. He will not, under any circumstance, take advantage of the tragic situation of the neighbor or a friend and seek to make money out of his misfortune.

In the days of the psalmist men borrowed money only when calamity had overtaken them and it was absolutely necessary to secure money to avert starvation or dire need. For the moment this good man, according to the psalmist, is utterly unwilling to enrich himself at the expense of some brother who is in a desperate plight.

This good man will, under no circumstance, be guilty of bribery. He will not allow money to influence him in dispensing judgment. He will not let his opinions be colored by any kind of consideration to the point where his eyes will be blinded to the truth. He will, under every circumstance, conduct himself as an honest gentleman who is determined to live and speak and have business relations with others on the basis of integrity and honesty. Following these interesting touches, the psalmist declares that he shall "never be moved."

Such a man will find himself selected by and welcomed by Jehovah himself. He will enjoy the full protection of Jehovah and enjoy forever the unshaken prosperity that comes when one is under the hand of God. His anchor holds, he shall not be moved. John said, "The world passeth away, and the lust thereof: but he that doeth the will of God abideth for ever" (1 John 2: 17). Jesus said, "No man is able to pluck them out of my Father's hand" (John 10: 29).

Other psalms add a special emphasis on kindness and

mercy, and declare that God's man is a kindly, considerate, generous soul, meek in heart, and continually seeking peace to pursue it. The psalmist declares that such a man shall inherit the land.

These Hebrew psalmists, while holding up a stern ideal and stressing a stern morality, dwelt much on the peace of mind that comes from a proper understanding of the divine will. The full holding of one's tongue, the keeping of sacred promises, dealing generously with neighbors and needy souls, and the kind of feeding on God's Word that would constantly keep the soul fed and nourished, will delight the heart of God.

Jesus, together with these psalmists, would remind us that character is something that comes as a result of God's touch upon us and that inner character will make for behavior that in every instance will bring joy to God's heart. It will, at the same time, provide the basis for behavior that will reveal us as God's men.

IV. Who Is Worthy? (Psalm 24)

He that hath clean hands, and a pure heart; who hath not lifted up his soul unto vanity, nor sworn deceitfully. He shall receive the blessing from the Lord, and righteousness from the God of his salvation.—Psalm 24: 4–5.

In the midst of a beautiful poem written to celebrate the entrance of the ark into Jerusalem after its capture by the forces under David's direction, we find four verses that describe the character of one who is to be an intimate associate of Jehovah. Who is worthy to enter God's holy presence?

One is reminded of the interesting story of Enoch and his walk with God. It is quite easy to let the imagination run for a bit and think on the qualities of soul and mind and personality that rendered Enoch such a good walking companion for God. Perhaps he was willing to take out of his life everything that could in any way displease God, and we may be sure that he was concerned with putting into his life everything that would add to the pleasure which God would get from association with him.

With those two elements securely grounded, perhaps we can study this little picture which David gives us of the moral character of one who is to enter God's house and become a constant friend and companion of the King.

In order to do this we must see something of the unique majesty of the One who was coming to take possession of his chosen house. It is Jehovah, God of hosts, whose sovereign power is not limited to any particular spot on earth. The entire world, every single inch of the earth's space, and all the creatures of the earth are his. He is the Creator and, as Creator, has the right to lay down all directions and laws and requirements that please him.

As the ark is brought up from its resting place to be deposited in a newly captured city, much thought and attention are given to the procession as the joyous subjects of the king bring themselves and all that they have into the celebration of this significant event.

The ark is far more than a mere cabinet or a box containing sacred reminders of God's presence. It represents God, and the poet let himself go in seeing the actual presence of God as he comes triumphantly to take over the city which is to be the actual heart of the capital and which will provide the heart-power that will bring Jehovah's people to him in adoration and worship and submission.

With this setting we will feel free to look into verses 3–6 to see what God's moral requirements are for one who is a chosen member of the select group to come in along with the ark. Let us remember that God's holiness and God's majesty are both to be considered in any statement of requirements or regulations. It is in the presence of the Holy One that they stand. It will be in his holy place that they are moving. What are the requirements for one who is so honored?

We stand in reverence as we see the high concepts revealed. Are we not prone to treat too lightly the privilege and responsibility of living in the presence of God?

1. All Men Want God

The question asked by the psalmist reveals the fact that deep in all men's hearts is an underlying desire to be close to God. All of us, wicked or good, would like to be eligible for that place. There is a consciousness in the hearts of men that they need him and need to be in his presence and to have those qualities of soul that will make them desirable as God looks through the list of men whom he has created. As the question is asked, we are reminded immediately that impure men are not in any way eligible. This involves the sense of sin, and the author of the psalm was conscious that since man is sinful there is no way by which he can enter the holy place and walk with the Holy One.

As the poet asks the question, "How can I enter?" he is dreading the answer, because seemingly there is no way to have the doors swing open for him. He is conscious of his great need of God. He is as conscious of the full whiteness of God's purity. He is becoming painfully aware of his own sinfulness; so with these considerations he inquires of God if there is any way that a sinful man can approach a holy God and satisfy the desires that are deepest in his soul. Perhaps all of us, at one time or another, can give expression to this same question and let our hearts beat a bit faster as we listen for the reply.

The psalmist would have us understand that God sits at the entrance of his tent and has a ready welcome for all that meet the qualifications. In some strange way the invitation goes out to all men. No one anywhere is excluded because of anything that is beyond him. When the requirements are stated and when the regulations are laid down, it will be seen that every individual on earth has an equal chance of gaining entrance to his side and becoming one of those who walks with the King.

The answer comes quickly, "He that hath clean hands, and a pure heart; who hath not lifted up his soul unto vanity, nor sworn deceitfully." Like a dash of cold water these four transcendently high requirements are spoken to the inquiring heart. How can one hope, ever, to measure up to this high demand? How can anyone anywhere dare believe that it is possible for his hands to be clean, his heart to be pure, and his allegiance complete? Where is the man who has measured up fully to these four qualifications?

2. A High Requirement

The poet found himself facing that question. According to the psalmist the man who is chosen is utterly innocent of all violence and every deed of wrongdoing. He is innocent in heart and mind and thought and purpose, as well as in deed. His soul has in every instance been true and faithful to Jehovah. He has never directed his mind toward or set his heart upon vanity, that which is false or unreal or transitory or sinful.

In addition to his relationship to God, the man has never sworn untruthfully in an attempt to deceive his neighbor. In short, he has been absolutely true to God and true to his fellow men. The psalmist is trying to say that absolute holiness is necessary. When we have faced honestly this statement of requirements, how can we be hopeful about approaching such a holy God and finding entrance into his presence?

It seems that the author has laid down a requirement that is impossible. He hastens, however, to say that "he shall receive the blessing from the Lord, and righteousness from the God of his salvation." The requirement that was utterly impossible before now becomes possible as God makes the divine gift and supplies that which the holy requirement had required. That which man could not produce, God has a way of giving. It almost seems that a great New Testament truth is breaking through, and that we can hear the words of Paul, "that I may . . . be found in him, not having my own righteousness, . . . but that which is of God through Christ" (Phil. 3: 9).

How marvelous it is that God makes possible that which otherwise would be utterly impossible! In our Lord Jesus Christ there is the forgiveness that blots out the past and a completely new life given by his own gracious hand, which in due time will develop the righteousness far beyond our reach. Instead of despair we have hope. He is providing that which otherwise we would never be able to reach. The blessings that can be enjoyed about the person of the Holy One will be ours as we have faith in him and commit our ways unto him and make him the Ruler of our hearts and lives and affections.

3. How May We Measure Up?

All these requirements, in each of these psalms, seem to be beyond our reach and too difficult to attain. Let us remember that in our day we are blessed not only by the example of Jesus, but by the new life which he makes possible in us when we accept him through faith and put our full trust in him. The old man is dead, the new man is a new creation through the power of the Saviour. The Holy Spirit comes in his own way to quicken and restore and guide and keep us in the way.

It seems impossible for an Old Testament saint to measure up to the difficult requirements of the psalmist. There should be no fear in our hearts that a newly born Christian can have the victory and live the victorious life, since we are new creatures and since Christ lives in us and since the Holy Spirit works through us.

Paul was daring in his statement, "We are more than conquerors through him that loved us" (Rom. 8: 37). Christ was reassuring in his word, "Lo, I am with you all the way." If there is in our hearts a great desire to walk with the King, let us not be afraid and let us not think of the requirements as being beyond our reach. But in simple faith let us lay hold on the promises of God and put our trust in the Saviour and walk triumphantly as the Holy Spirit leads, knowing that moral qualities such as the Old Testament prescribes are qualities that are natural in one who is a born-again Christian. We will rejoice in victories and will delight in knowing that other victories are to be ours as we go from height to height, trusting him who makes us "more than conquerors."

CHAPTER II

THANKSGIVING AND SHOUTING

IN THE GARDEN of our hearts there is one flower that is sadly neglected. We may grow many fine specimens and show them off to our friends with eagerness and with pardonable pride, but when someone discovers the fact that we have not given a place in the garden of our hearts for the flower called gratitude, we will probably be greatly embarrassed. One of the richest notes in all the songs of a Christian's heart is the note of gratitude which gives forth thanksgiving to God, not only for his mercy, but for his wise rule over the earth.

If we could but stop and think through all of the reasons why gratitude should well up within our hearts and grow as a beautiful flower in the garden of our souls, perhaps we would become overwhelmed at the full reach of God's goodness to us. The personal gifts he makes, the special mercies he gives us, and the intimate lift which comes to us as individuals would come in for a hurried accounting; but if we should launch forth, as the psalmist does, into all of the reaches of God's goodness and mercy to all peoples and toward the fulfilment of his plan and purpose for the world, we would realize more adequately some of the basic reasons for gratitude.

The psalmist is foremost in his emphasis upon thanksgiving and praise and gratitude. All the way through the book of Psalms we are constantly brought back to that note of praise and thanksgiving. Many sections of Psalms are completely filled with words expressing this inner thankfulness.

In a brief study it would be impossible for us to cover all of those that are most typical and call to mind the ones that lend themselves most beautifully to interpretation and application. We will endeavor, as best we can, to look for a moment into Psalms 9, 47, 103, 116, and perhaps others in that great list toward the end of the Psalter.

May this study fan to fresh flame smoldering embers of gratitude, that our lives may glow anew with thanksgiving.

I. GOD'S UNBOUNDED LOVE (PSALM 9: 1–2)

I will praise thee, O Lord, with my whole heart; I will shew forth all thy marvellous works.—Psalm 9: 1.

In this psalm the author takes up almost the exact lines with which he closed Psalm 7 and declares that it is his joy to pour forth all of the praise that is at his command. Joyful strains rend the air as heart and soul and all his being take part in this concentration of shouting and praising the eternal God who has demonstrated his power, his might, his wisdom, and his divine love. He recognizes that such gifts as God has put out upon his people call for thankful acknowledgment and joyful confession. It is his joy, as a recipient, to record his thanksgiving to God for his wondrous deeds.

These deeds are beyond any dream of those who ask because they are beyond human comprehension. As long as he lives, he will shout aloud the praise of God who has brought about these signal deliverances. With his mouth and with his heart he will laud the name of the most High. It is a pure bit of praise.

The first line perhaps could best be translated, "I will give thanks unto the Lord." He is pouring out all the praise of his heart that he can gather up, because it is in his great purpose and in his plan. He is sure that love has prompted all of it.

It is not only something that has already been accomplished that brings the most joy, but the realization that this God who has so bountifully poured out his blessings will continue throughout all the ages to respond in the same manner to importunate prayer. The poet will not only pray and thank, but he will hope for even richer gifts in the years ahead. It is his own beloved Father God who has given such a demonstration of power and mercy.

Such praise demands the whole heart, the integration of the whole personality in a great symphony of thanksgiving and testimony. The song begins with praise for God's works, but soon it advances and the rejoicing is directed toward God himself, and toward his name.

II. THE KING OF ALL THE EARTH (PSALM 47: 1, 6)

O clap your hands, all ye people; shout unto God with the voice of triumph. . . . Sing praises to God, sing praises: sing praises unto our King, sing praises.—Psalm 47: 1, 6.

Psalm 47 has gained a real place of importance in the interest of the people as they have associated it with the ascension of Christ. If we study it fully we can find the kind of prophetical meaning that would fit it for such an occasion.

As a matter of fact, the psalm itself was identified completely with an occurrence in the time of Jehoshaphat when Jehovah came in such signal way to deliver his people from a terrible invasion that threatened to engulf their land and destroy all vestige of life and kingdom. The psalmist breaks forth in praise, in rejoicing, in shouting. The signal victory gained by Jehovah was not a victory that consisted in bloody subjection and death among enemies, but the real victory was in changing the hearts of the nations of the earth so that they could worship him with joy and gladness.

The psalm reaches its climax in the beautiful line, "For God is the King of all the earth." That idea is reasonably old with us and perhaps a bit commonplace, but in the psalmist's day and throughout the Old Testament it was a revolutionary idea that must have thrilled the worshipers of Jehovah to the depths of their beings. No wonder the psalmist declares that all peoples must join him in praise to the One who has not only won a victory over earthly foes, but has had the power to establish himself as the King of all the earth.

Those who would see in this a picture of the ascension of Christ picture the Lord Jesus as coming and laying aside his heavenly glory and engaging in mortal combat with the enemies of God. After he has conquered the enemies, he finds himself eligible for the praise and worship and adoration of all peoples. He ascends to his heavenly home to put on the robes of glory and majesty again and to take his place to rule among the peoples of the earth. These people are called from all parts of the world to bow their knees before him and to raise their shouts of praise and thanksgiving.

III. PERSONAL TRIUMPHS (PSALM 116)

> *Gracious is the Lord, and righteous; yea, our God is merciful. . . . For the Lord hath dealt bountifully with thee. For thou hast delivered my soul from death, mine eyes from tears, and my feet from falling. . . . I will offer to thee the sacrifice of thanksgiving, and will call upon the name of the Lord.*—Psalm 116: 5, 7–8, 17.

The author of this psalm has suffered a severe illness and has been in the very jaws of death. Perhaps physicians and friends gave him up except for some friends who remained by his side praying. We are told that he prayed with faith, even against all odds. This psalm is a glorious shout of thanksgiving because of deliverance from the illness that was already ushering him into the realm of the dead.

Perhaps you have never experienced such an illness. Maybe you have not faced the stark certainty of the end of this life. If you have it may be that you can enter reasonably deep into an understanding of what this psalmist experienced.

Whatever else we may say about him, the psalmist had bushels of gratitude well up within him that came pouring forth in shouts of thanksgiving and in the purest praise. He is so joyful and so happy in the realization that God has done this that he breaks forth in a declaration of his love for him. After all that is fundamental and basic. If God, by this signal act, was able to bring about a state of sincere and whole-hearted love, a real miracle was performed.

He declares then that he will praise God as long as he lives, and he mentions some of the things God has done for him. First of all, when he prayed, God inclined his ear; second, he heard his voice; third, he delivered him; and, fourth, he dealt bountifully with him. We can hardly realize in those simple statements all that was involved in the psalmist's words, but if we pause on each of them and let the whole thought sink in, we will realize that the psalmist was telling of some rather miraculous things that came to him.

Not only is he willing to keep on praising God and to pour out thanksgiving, as long as he lives, but he declares that he is going to do some other things. His love for God and his gratitude to him will prompt him to do something for the One he loves. First of all, he declares, "I will take the cup of salvation." Second, "I will . . . call upon the name of the Lord." Third, "I will walk before the Lord." Fourth, "I will pay my vows unto the Lord now." Fifth, "I will praise the Lord." The promises there are not too much for God to ask of any one of us who has been delivered from any of the catastrophes that beset our way.

The psalmist knows perfectly well that in this experience he has received blessings the value of which no one can estimate. He knows that these blessings are worth more to him than all of the things that life could possibly give him. He is now ready, in his own humble way, to pour out to his loving Father God everything that he has in his possession. It will be a joy, both privately and publicly, to continue his thanksgiving by work and also by deed.

Gratitude impels the author of this psalm to express in thought, in word, and in deed the deep response of his overflowing heart. Everywhere he goes men will hear his story and know that now he is in love with God and that he has dedicated the best in love and service to the One who has done so much for him. It seems to the psalmist that anything short of that kind of dedication is a rather poor way of expressing gratitude.

Perhaps the psalmist has a word for us in our generation. Not only could we pause to express our thanks, but on bended knee we could dedicate ourselves wholly and completely to the One who has thus rewarded us and to the One who has made us indebted to him for life.

The word *hallelujah* at the close of the psalm, is an interesting word. He is calling upon all peoples to unite with him and to make his solo of praise a glorious choral anthem. The word *hallelu* is a Hebrew verb in the imperative, and it is

translated "praise ye." The word *Jah* is Jehovah or Lord, so
we have *hallelu-jah*. All peoples are urged to unite their
voices and their whole lives in helping him praise the One
who so richly deserves all the praise of which men are capable.

IV. BLESS THE LORD (PSALM 103)

> *Bless the Lord, O my soul; and all that is within me,*
> *bless his holy name. Bless the Lord, O my soul, and forget*
> *not all his benefits: who forgiveth all thine iniquities;*
> *who healeth all thy diseases; who redeemeth thy life from*
> *destruction; who crowneth thee with lovingkindness and*
> *tender mercies; who satisfieth thy mouth with good things;*
> *so that thy youth is renewed like the eagle's. . . . The*
> *Lord is merciful and gracious, slow to anger, and plen-*
> *teous in mercy. . . . Bless the Lord, O my soul.*—Psalm
> 103: 1–5, 8, 22.

The most beautiful, the most perfect, the most comprehensive, of all the psalms of thanksgiving is the one we now
endeavour to interpret. Who has not been thrilled by the
words, "Bless the Lord, O my soul: and all that is within me,
bless his holy name"? For well on to three thousand years
men and women, boys and girls, have recited those beautiful
words.

When a man finds a God whose character satisfies his
moral sense completely, whose wisdom satisfies all of the demands of his mind, and whose love completely satisfies the
desires of his heart, nothing further could be asked. Seemingly one who enters fully into the pronouncement of these
two lovely lines has done just that.

Surely the author of this psalm had come into a full understanding of God and, knowing him, he was completely satisfied with every side of his nature. There were no defects,
there were no shortcomings, nothing failed to measure up to
the highest of his dreams and standards.

The psalmist was a pure man whose heart was capable of
sensing spiritual depths. He was a humble man in the presence of God and God's mercies. He could see and understand

the full nature of sin so completely that God's own conception seemed to be as natural as the simplest fact about him. He knew how God hated sin and in that knowledge dared invite all his neighbors and friends to submit to the moral surgery that alone could give life and joy and peace.

He was a mighty master of divine revelation, knowing history and law and poetry and prophecy and recognizing revelation's value in causing others to know and appreciate salvation. He was constantly concerned that men might become acquainted with God through the means he has provided.

The psalmist's knowledge of God's will for men sprang from a keen insight and breadth of affection and a grasp of the central theme of the New Testament so that he was equipped as a spiritual giant to interpret God not only as a mighty warrior with mailed fist and stern countenance and a victorious might, but as a loving Father whose heart is love and who delights to hear the cry of one of his children. These truths about God and about God's revelation made him thoroughly capable of leading not only his own soul, but the peoples of the earth and all succeeding generations to shout forth praises to this loving Father God.

The psalm falls into the following outline:

In verses 1–5 the poet calls upon his own soul to tell of God's individual gifts to him, gifts that include justification, redemption, and renewing grace.

In verses 6–10 we are given some clear illustrations of God's goodness to Israel.

Verses 11–14 picture God as a God of love who delights to forgive.

In verses 15–18 man is pictured as a person who lives but a brief moment compared with the eternity of the existence of the eternal God.

In verses 19–22 the psalmist gathers up all of his strength and calls on all peoples, all creatures, everything that can possibly join in the chorus of praise and adoration. To close the psalm he calls upon himself to join enthusiastically and joyously in a personal shout of thanksgiving.

Truly the Holy Spirit inspired this unusual man of God to record for us the challenge that will never lose its freshness and will never be out of date. He would speak to your heart and to mine today urging us to think on God's goodness and mercy and then rejoice in the privilege of shouting our praises to him.

1. Counting His Blessings

After the psalmist has given us that immortal opening sentence, "Bless the Lord, O my soul: and all that is within me, bless his holy name," he begins counting the blessings that God has so generously given. He speaks of sin and man's need for forgiveness. Forgiveness stands at the head of the list of God's gifts. Step by step he goes through the list of those things which are divine gifts to one who is now grateful for them.

God gladly and willingly forgives, heals, redeems, crowns, satisfies, and renews. Plenteous grace is behind each of these gifts. Sin must be removed, and God has sufficient grace to remove it. Disease is not in keeping with God's will for one whom he loves, and so disease must be destroyed, and so on through a long list the psalmist recounts the blessings of a loving God. Let us begin with these and think on them for a moment.

2. He Forgives

His first gift from God which calls for gratitude is divine forgiveness. He understands fully how sin has wounded and warped and ruined his better self. He knows perfectly well that nothing in all man's supply can possibly remove the stains of sin. When he called on God, God gladly and generously forgave.

Do you wonder that this gratitude which came so spontaneously is now expressed as the purest praise in the light of the marvelous gift which he has received from a loving God? That note is the deepest note in all true worship. When a man sees and understands the depths of the love of God, he immediately becomes conscious of the fact that he stands in need of forgiveness. When he sees and understands the mercy that God has available and that God stands ready to forgive, his heart can do no other than burst out in song and praise and thanksgiving.

Let us pause for a moment to record our own debt of sincere thanks to God for coming in a moment when sin had a grip on our hearts and when in sheer desperation we lifted our hands to him and begged for forgiveness. He came with the swiftness and with the loving touch that could only be the gift of a loving Father and not only redeemed us from sin, but forgave us fully and cleansed us from every taint of the sin that was upon us.

The psalmist is but speaking that which is uppermost in the heart and mind of so many of us who can look back to that holy moment when our sins were forgiven and when they were carried away and remembered against us no more. How wondrous was the Gift! How spontaneous ought to be our praise and thanksgiving!

3. He Heals

The author of this psalm begins the next line by declaring that God is not only One who forgives sins, but he has healed his disease. The psalmist declares that those diseases that were wrecking his life and making him utterly miserable and causing the kind of suffering of mind and spirit that made a wreck of him, under the touch of the Great Physician have been fully healed.

How many are the occasions in your life and mine, and in the lives of so many of our friends and neighbors, when God has touched with his divine fingers and healed physical diseases or restored peace and quiet and serenity to the human mind, and brought peace of soul so that one could rest quietly and serenely in the arms of a loving Father God? What a marvelous boon it is to have One to heal!

We appreciate physcians and nurses and drugs and remedies that are man-made, but we must recognize that the healing of body and mind and spirit is the work of a loving Father. Many of us ought at this very moment to pause and shout aloud our praise and our thanksgiving and to record once and for all our deep gratitude to the One who has healed all these diseases!

4. He Redeems

The author continues by saying that he "redeems my life from destruction." It is difficult to know just what is included in that statement. We are sure that in some deep, dark moment in his life a tragedy was averted, a calamity was pushed aside. He was snatched, as it were, from the very jaws of death. Surely his heart would cry out in thanksgiving.

It is so easy for us to forget that all the way through from early babyhood days we have been walking miracles. How often, when we have been least aware of it, we have been delivered by the hand of God from some serious accident or destruction? In Psalm 34, verse 7, the poet says, "The angel of the Lord encampeth round about them that fear him, and delivereth them." How awe-inspiring! How vivid! How heart-lifting it is to know that our lives so often have been lifted out of the very jaws of destruction by One who watches, One who loves, One who is all powerful, One who has taken peculiar delight in redeeming our lives from destruction.

5. He Crowns

The psalmist declares that he was grateful to God because in his life he has been crowned with loving-kindness. How often have you been crowned? Has it occurred to you that all through your days, even though earthly rulers failed to crown you, God has come each morning and placed on your brow the crown of loving-kindness?

His grace, rich, full, plenteous, has been his gift to you. As the day has worn on, his crown has been made more beautiful in moments of need, as well as in moments of rejoicing.

His crown has been the gift of the loving Father who by that means has given evidence of his divine approval and his love for you.

6. He Satisfies

Again the psalmist declares that he "satisfieth thy desire with good things." Satisfaction is a wondrous gift. How many people are genuinely satisfied? How many remedies satisfy us fully? How often does our food or our lodging or our treatment from friends or neighbors or employers bring the fullest satisfaction? Who is able to claim that in all things he is completely satisfied? The psalmist recognizing that yearning for satisfaction declares that his God is a God who constantly brings the deepest and richest satisfaction. Surely something ought to be said by way of thanksgiving to a God who completely satisfies the deepest yearnings of the soul of a man. Have you expressed your gratitude?

7. He Renews

And then in a line which is strangely colorful he said, "Thy youth is renewed like the eagle's." One of the greatest desires of human beings is to continue young. Medicine makers have become rich providing those things which promise to ward off old age and feeble years. Have you had a yearning for the fountain of youth? Have you looked longingly at advertisements that tell you of their claims to keep you young in feelings as well as in looks?

Listen to Isaiah as he said, "They that wait for Jehovah shall renew their strength, they shall mount up with wings as eagles; they shall run, and not be weary; they shall walk, and not faint" (40: 31 ASV). The psalmist has found the secret, and he has come openly and continually to the One who renews his youth and now he is telling his soul of that special gift from God. He calls on his soul to prostrate itself in humility and to shout aloud his praises for One who is so merciful.

8. His Wondrous Works

The psalmist goes on a bit further to say, "Jehovah exe-cuteth righteous acts, and judgments for all that are oppressed. He made known his ways unto Moses, his doings unto the children of Israel" (ASV). He knows perfectly well that God in his infinite mercy has also been a God of judgment and righteousness and that he has been a God who has ruled all the areas of the earth. His will has been that all men should come under his sway and be blessed from his hand.

The psalmist knows Mosaic history. He has read the story of the powerful right hand of the most High stretched out to deliver his people. He knows that in these historical psalms he has been watching the triumphant tread of one who is above all and who is working out his plan in the ages. He knows that it is quite easy to take the short look and see but just a small bit of God's ruling and then misjudge because so little of this span of eternity is visible.

In the face of it all he is thoroughly alive to the fact that God brings about justice in the earth, that God is taking his own good time about working out his plans and his programs, that sometimes it seems altogether too long, but that justice will prevail and righteousness will have its way. He knows that the God to whom he is bowing in humble worship is the God who will rule all the earth and all men shall be brought under his sway.

In our own day perhaps we too have lost sight of the fact that "God moves in a mysterious way his wonders to perform." Maybe we have become impatient and have failed to see that God can be trusted to put a muzzle on all the human wild beasts who are set to destroy the earth. Perhaps someday we can come as this psalmist to take the long look and realize that as the Bible revealed it to us God is a God who does not seek to settle all matters within a brief span, but that in his own way and in his own time, he is working it all out. The psalmist finds much in that thought to cause him to thank God and to trust him more implicitly for the days ahead.

If we could see and understand that God is having his way and that God will continually drive toward the full completion of his purpose and plan, we could have more joy in our hearts and less fear, and we could in quietness lean on him and recognize that the One who created the earth and who has ruled through all of the centuries is still ruling and reigning and that his way is to be the way of righteousness and victory. Surely we too can rejoice and praise him.

9. His Inexhaustible Love

The psalmist has found that God is full of compassion and "gracious, slow to anger, and abundant in lovingkindness." He understands something of the great love of God that is exhaustless in its treasures dealt out to those who are his own. God's anger may be visible for brief moments, because even the best child needs the chastening hand of God, but if the anger flames for a moment, the flame of love and mercy continues without ceasing, and the mercy which shows lovingkindness is unending. He goes on to say that he is sure that God has never punished Israel as much as she deserved.

If we could become acquainted with the infinite grace of God, we would see something of what the psalmist was facing as he looked into the very heart of God and realized that such relationship, being a filial relationship, demanded the most outspoken thanksgiving and praise.

As he goes forward, in verses 11–14, the psalmist is describing for us in further words the tenderness of the Lord's forgiving love. He reaches as far as it is possible for his human mind to reach into infinite space, and then with all space made a part of the towering height of God's mercy, the psalmist is almost out of breath as he thinks of some way of expressing love for and devotion to the One who has done so much and who now is the kind of Father God who will help. In the development of that idea he has declared that he has had compassion on us, that man is frail, but God, the One who formed him and made him for himself, is the One who is most devoted to him. Even as a loving Father he understands every weakness and every frailty and in the midst of it all he comes to bless.

The fatherhood of God, so beautifully pictured in this psalm, is but a thought that is to develop and grow even sweeter under the touch of Jesus' teaching. He came to make it clear, in his picture of the prodigal son, how earnestly and yearningly the father longs for the privilege of ministering to his wayward boy, and how great is the joy about the throne of God when one who has wandered comes home. The psalmist is in possession of the essence of this idea and so this throws him into a new avalanche of praise and thanksgiving.

10. His Eternal Existence

To make the picture complete, in verses 15–18, the author tells us that man has very little hope of continuing in the midst of so many difficult situations and tragic experiences, but Jehovah's loving-kindness and righteousness will endure forever and ever. The eternity of God is the rock upon which faith rests its weary head in the sight of failing humanity that can hope for nothing better than an early end to life's fitful way.

The psalmist, while he does not have a fully worked-out theory of the future life, has at least the joy of knowing that his case is in the hand of a Father God who loves, who forgives, who will forever have in mind those frail creatures who without him would be utterly insufficient.

As the psalmist wraps his mind around this idea, he is lifted into ecstasies at the thought that whether in this life or the next, his case is wholly in the hands of a loving Father who knows him, who formed him, who has watched over him as an earthly father would watch a frail child, who will in every emergency be present to lift and bless, who will in eternity continue to be the same great forgiving God whose delight will be to provide that which a soul needs throughout the endless ages that will stretch before him.

The depths of the riches of these verses stagger us and cause us to realize that the psalmist had a good reason for thanking God. His source for gratitude was well founded. For one who could think of God in terms like these, surely thanksgiving was in order.

What could happen to you or me to bring about this deep conception of God and his infinite mercy? How could you be brought to sense the love of God so that your life might be completely aware always of this infinite love so that the streams of gratitude would run unceasingly? That seems to be the essence of the psalmist's desire as he speaks his word to succeeding generations. It is almost too much for his heart. He wants to share with others not only the depth of his knowledge, but something of the feeling which runs so deep within his own heart. He is shouting his praise, pouring forth his thanks, speaking his deep gratitude.

11. A Call to All Creatures to Praise

As the psalmist sweeps into his closing paragraph, he seems to recognize God in such sublime fashion that he senses that his authority, his sovereignty, is both universal and that he, having established his throne in heaven, is worthy of mightier praise than one little psalmist is capable of. So he calls on all creation to join him in this burst of praise, "Bless Jehovah, ye angels of his, ye mighty in strength that do his word, hearken unto the voice of his word."

All the heavenly beings are capable of praising the heavenly King so the poet calls on all of them, young and old, high and low, everywhere in heaven, on the earth, wherever men can utter a syllable.

The theme the psalmist has is now too great for a solo. It must be sung by a great chorus. The sons of men are not sufficient for the mighty theme, so he calls with all his voice upon celestial beings to join in this exalted chorus, this anthem of praise, this shout of thanksgiving. He feels somehow that he has moved so far in his spiritual steppings that he can actually get the ear of the celestial beings, and he would like to have every created thing turn into a great musical instrument to swell this chorus of praise.

Then the psalmist closes with that same note on which he started, "Bless the Lord, O my soul." He somehow comes back to that point from which he started in this universal hymn of praise. He wants to have his part, however humble, and to join his own voice as triumphantly as he can in a shout that will reverberate around the earth and reach to the very portals of heaven, because out of sheer gratitude his heart is speaking.

From a clear conception of what love has done for him he is telling his appreciation. From the fullest understanding of the mighty power and the fatherly love of God he wants a part in announcing something of the depths of his rejoicing.

V. An Anthem of Praise (Psalm 100)

Whether we know the one hundredth Psalm or not, practically every one of us knows the lines that we call the doxology,

> Praise God, from whom all blessings flow;
> Praise Him all creatures here below;
> Praise Him above, ye heavenly host;
> Praise Father, Son, and Holy Ghost.

We are aware of the fact that those lines mean much in the worship in the churches. This psalm found its way into the very worship ritual. In some way it seems to sum up and become the climax of all the songs of praise. William Kethe, in 1561, wrote paraphrase that has been a blessing to millions of hearts.

> All people that on earth do dwell,
>   Sing to the Lord with cheerful voice;
> Him serve with fear, His praise forth tell;
>   Come before Him and rejoice.
>
> Know that the Lord is God indeed;
>   Without our aid he did us make;
> We are His flock, He doth us feed,
>   And for His sheep he doth us take.

1. Imperatives for Praise

In this marvelous hymn of praise there are seven promi-
nent verbs: *shout, serve, come, know, enter, thank, bless*. If
you will put a circle around those seven verbs and then realize
that they are great imperatives for our heart, perhaps you
will be impressed with the realization that this psalmist is
vitally concerned about impressing your heart and mine with
the one great opportunity that we have of shouting aloud
our thanksgiving and understanding properly our debt to
the eternal One. He is the one who has created us, who has
redeemed us, who loves us with his great love, who has a
mighty purpose for us, and who has made provisions for us
at the end of the journey.

Any one of these blessings would be sufficient to cause us
to praise the Lord forever. The fact that we are creatures of
his very hand and, therefore, wholly and completely indebted to him for the life we breathe, and that he loved us
sufficiently to give his only begotten Son to die on the cross
that we might have life, ought to break our hearts and cause
us to fall at his feet and love him with all the love of which
we are capable.

If we could one time sense the matchless love that not only
drove the Lord Jesus to the cross, but has continued to mani-
fest itself in every day of our lives, we would dedicate all that
we have to him. His love for us is an unceasing love, without
wavering or failing, without forgetting us or neglecting us,
without in any way losing sight of the wondrous gifts he has
for each of us. He continues on and on to give and to bless
and to prepare us for the eternal joys that await us.

If we could, however, understand anything like the marvel
of God's purpose for us, both in this life and on the other
shore, we would be disposed to fall lovingly and humbly at
his feet, to prostrate ourselves not only in worship, but to
arise to pour out thanksgiving as long as there is breath left
for us. If we could see for one flitting moment the provisions
he has made for us on the other shore, we, too, would be disposed to come as the psalmist came and not only thank him

ourselves, but call upon everyone everywhere to enter into his gates with thanksgiving and into his courts with praise.

2. *Make Our Places of Worship Joyous*

We will, if we are true Christians, seek in the best way possible to make our places of worship joyous meeting places where light and radiance and joyfulness and thankfulness have their place. We will see that a distressed soul can come and find the lift that will send him out with a new spring in his step, with a new light in his eye, with a new joy in his heart, with a new determination to live his life for the Lord. We have such a great responsibility.

The Lord has laid upon us the privilege and the responsibility of conducting the worship services whether we stand on the platform or have a place of prominence in the building, or whether we are one individual taking a special place of quiet worship. We may be sure that upon us falls the responsibility of helping lift the very atmosphere into a genuine praise and anthem for God. When we enter God's house, it ought to be in this spirit. All our lives ought to be beautiful and made wondrously Christlike by the gratitude that wells up within us.

Chapter III

THE GOOD SHEPHERD

When we look carefully at the twenty-third Psalm, we are face to face with one of the sublime creations of all time. When they tell us of the Seven Wonders of the World, they do not mention this psalm. When they list the great creations of literature, even in the spiritual realm, sometimes they leave this one out, but surely it is the pearl of the book of Psalms. It is the first one that a child learns, the one he repeats most often as he grows up, the one he remembers longest, the one his thick lips repeat in the last moment of his life. It is more than three thousand years old and yet so new, so colorful, so adapted to our every need that it could well have come from the pen of God this morning.

The little child learns to repeat it at his mother's knee. The great Old Testament scholar spends weeks and months and even years working on each of the Hebrew words and seeking from cognate languages the hidden meaning wrapped in its words. In the church service the voice of the minister speaks forth its words, and the entire audience becomes still and listens to its matchless message. The old man, whether well or ill, listens as it is read or feeds on it as his own eyes follow the words. When the end of life comes and the shadows darken about one, the choice of all would be these blessed words of David.

These words tell us of the Shepherd who gave his life for the sheep. They paint for us the picture of green pastures and still waters. They describe for us rough, rugged paths of righteousness that must be endured. They unroll before us the picture of the valley of the shadow, and before we have followed this psalmist to the end of the verse, we are rejoicing that the valley of the shadow becomes an avenue to God and to his home.

These words describe for us, too, faithful guardians who walk at our heels to make possible safety, security, and effectiveness. We are brought face to face with the cheering realization that there is a home at the end of the journey, prepared by the loving hand of God himself and made ready for our individual occupancy.

Someone has said that verse 1 tells us of a person, verse 2 of a provision, verse 3 of a pathway, verse 4 of a peril, verse 5 of a preparation, and verse 6 of a prospect. Whatever may be said in arranging these verses or these ideas in interesting lines, we are still unable to fathom the full meaning or understand all that the Holy Spirit had in mind when he inspired David to give us these words. In them we have a divine assurance of nourishment, refreshment, rest, guidance, restoration, protection, comfort, permanence, pardon, provision, and prospect. All the way through the psalmist is depicting for us the wonders of God's provision for those who love him and for those who are so loved by the divine One.

I. The Author

Perhaps we should take a few moments to think on the author himself. Six short verses like these after two thousand years and after they have sung their way into hundreds of millions of homes, and after they have revealed the true beauty of such a supreme classic to our own hearts, challenge us.

We would like to know not only about the Saviour, who is pictured, but about the man who is the human author of these words. Of course, the Holy Spirit is the real author, because no human being could have produced such marvelous array of image and word and picture and character of God.

David's faith is sublime trust in God. His serenity is as clear and placid as God's infinite assurance. The psalm tells of darkness and enemies and mountain defiles and gorges of sorrow and distress and disappointment, but it tells also of a Shepherd who walks with him, whose one purpose is to find food for his flock and to protect them from beast and robbers. How helpless are the sheep without him! No life could last very long without the Shepherd to feed and to protect. With him they are secure and without any need of fear or discouragement.

The psalmist is evidently a man of mature years who has suffered a great deal, who has been in dangerous places, who has known what it is to rely upon God in hours of peril, in hours of almost certain death, who has realized what it is to have implacable foes at his heels, who has understood something of the loneliness and isolation of desert or wilderness life, who loves the hills of home, and who longs with all his heart for a protector, a guide, a loving God.

David evidently wrote this poem late in his life, after having experienced all of these tragic hours and after coming into a quiet confidence, a serene sunlight, a joyous faith, and after realizing that his God was like a shepherd in every particular. He has found him to be the ideal Shepherd who cares for, who loves, who provides food for, who protects, who leads, who finally brings the sheep safely to the home where joys unspeakable can be shared.

Being a shepherd, David knows his sheep as individuals. He has a special attachment for every one of them. He can call each one by his own name. When one of them is lost, he has gone willingly and enthusiastically after him, and then the rejoicing has been in his own heart and from his lips. He knows what it is to guide the sheep by the right paths into the area where a bit of grass can be found, even in a very dry land, and where an occasional oasis is available for water to keep the grass green and to provide a little pool by the side of which the sheep may eat and drink and rest. He has gone often to such a place with his own flock.

David realizes perfectly well that God has done that for him often and that in the remaining years of his life he expects God to do exactly that for him. We love him for his beautiful picture of the life of a shepherd. Jesus must have loved this psalm as he learned it, no doubt, from his mother's knee. From the beginning of his ministry he visualized himself as the Good Shepherd, and freely accepted that costly ministry.

II. The Setting

As we try to unfold the meaning of the psalm, we must realize that it is set in a background of unrest, confusion, hostility, weariness, poverty, hard journeying, perplexing problems, actual dangers, deep valleys, cruel enemies, and a constant thought on what is beyond in the infinite area of God's own presence.

When David comes to find God as a Good Shepherd, somehow he is able to cancel out a great deal of that which was forbidding. Instead of weariness God provides pastures and still waters and rest. When he is being subjected to severe disciplines, he hears the Master say, "I am with thee." When he is in perplexing situations and is unable to decide which way to move, he realizes that the Shepherd is a guide and that he knows which is the right way. When he comes to have fear rising up within his throat and seeking to strangle him, he is suddenly aware of the presence of God who chases fear from his presence.

Even his vilest enemies are made to look like pygmies when David realizes that God is near. When he is hardest put to provide food to sustain him in dire distress he suddenly realizes that God is his Host, that he provides a superabundance of that which is life-giving. When he thinks most wistfully of the end of his life journey and wonders most interestingly of the tangled woods in which it seems to be leading, he is suddenly awakened to the realization that his Shepherd has a home at the end of the way, and that when life's journey is over he will be ushered into the presence of the Good Shepherd who has watched over him and kept him through the years.

III. The Shepherd

How could one in Old Testament days, a thousand years before the coming of Christ, without the benefit of most of the Old Testament and all of the New, without the benefit of the teachings of the Lord Jesus, come into such a holy conception of those things which matter most to the human heart?

Everything that has to do with the human life is dealt with by this Shepherd. David identifies him as One who completely deals with the problem of rest and weariness, who deals adequately with the problem of hunger and bodily need, who in a masterful way defeats and eliminates fear, who makes even dark valleys become light and beautiful because of the actual presence of the Good Shepherd. David can jump over all of the theological decisions of his day and project himself through the power of the Holy Spirit into a New Testament conception of this home at the end of the journey alongside of the Good Shepherd himself.

We do not wonder that Jesus, in presenting his most appealing picture of himself, took up this thousand-year-old poem of only six verses and poured his own divine contribution into it and revealed in language that we can never forget that the Good Shepherd gives his life for his sheep. In Old Testament theology a sheep and a lamb were killed for the shepherd. Jesus' blessed contribution will be that the shepherd offers his life fully and freely for the sheep.

So you see it is all bound up together and made beautiful together, because the Holy Spirit, who was speaking in the ear and heart of David, is the same One who today reveals the hidden meaning of this truth to our own hearts. He is our interpreter. He takes these three-thousand-year-old words and makes clear and lucid and unforgettable the message for all our hearts.

IV. THE INFLUENCE OF THIS PSALM

Eternity alone can reveal all of the sacred influences that have been set in motion by this beautiful poem. All of the multitudes who are gathered round about the throne will have in their hearts a shout of praise to David, the immortal author of these words. He listened as the Holy Spirit spoke and then in his own simple mountain Hebrew put them down, an ageless, a timeless, an eternal message that not only has truth in it to the very last inch, but has the simplicity of expression, the sweetness of meaning, and the directness of approach that has made men of all races and all ages see in it a picture of the shepherd of the sheep who wanted to be the Shepherd of each one of us. It pictures God in love with his people, with rest in his bosom, with grace for all our needs, with comfort and joy in sorrow, with a message of hope so sweet and clear that the music breaks forth from the soul.

> *The Lord is my shepherd; I shall not want. He maketh me to lie down in green pastures: he leadeth me beside the still waters. He restoreth my soul: he leadeth me in the paths of righteousness for his name's sake. Yea, though I walk through the valley of the shadow of death, I will fear no evil: for thou art with me; thy rod and thy staff they comfort me. Thou preparest a table before me in the presence of mine enemies: thou anointest my head with oil; my cup runneth over. Surely goodness and mercy shall follow me all the days of my life: and I will dwell in the house of the Lord for ever.*—Psalm 23.

1. "I Shall Not Want"

When David says, "The Lord is my shepherd; I shall not want," he is definitely claiming God as his very own. We almost shudder as we realize the audacity of a man who dares claim God as his very own, and yet that is exactly what David did and that is what we can do without the slightest hesitation, because he has made it clear to us that we are to claim him as our own, even as he claims us as his own, if we have given our hearts to him.

When David says, "I do not want" or "I shall not want," he is saying definitely that with the Lord as his Shepherd and with these two lovely bodyguards ("goodness" and "mercy") following directly behind and with eternity wide open for him, he knows perfectly well that there need be no thought of want along the way.

Are you thrilled to think that all your wants can be supplied in the Shepherd? Every need of body or mind or spirit or time or eternity is fully and bountifully supplied in him. That is what David is trying to say. He leaves nothing out. Since he has God as his own Shepherd, there is nothing beyond the reach of his praying.

Jesus made it even stronger when in John he declared, "If ye shall ask any thing in my name, I will do it" (14: 14) and "Ye shall ask what ye will, and it shall be done unto you" (15: 7).

It is a great joy to know that we, in our own limited station in life, can claim that same remarkable assurance, and since he is our Shepherd, there need be no fear of any need going unfilled. It is his delight, his joy to do all of that for those who are his.

2. Rest and Refreshment

David continues by declaring that God gently guides him into the place of food and sustenance and nourishment and refreshment and rest. We could easily spend a long while thinking on the Palestinian shepherd and his sheep in a very dry area where few patches of grass and fewer pools of water were available. It was a hard life, both for the sheep and for the shepherd. Loving them as he did, the shepherd sought diligently to find grass that would sustain and water that would refresh them and to provide, along with these two needs, rest in the heat of the day.

David declares that Jehovah does just that for him. He, of course, is using the figure that was most familiar to him as a shepherd outside Bethlehem, but he was describing in detail God's provisions for him and God's eternal provisions for all who are his.

In a world where so many of us get the idea that we are independent, it is difficult to give proper place to God's loving care in providing food and nourishment and refreshment and rest. It is his delight as it is the delight of a loving mother or father to provide the very best in every way for the growing child. We are his children and he loves us with an infinite love. He knows better than any earthly parent would know what is needed to provide the best of growth and the best of sustenance.

David declares that God delights to do all of those things and that as long as life lasts for us, God will be at that task of providing the things that our physical bodies need, the things that our minds need, the things that we need in the way of restoration and strength and hospitalization and vitamins and rest cures, and everything else that is needed to make life the abundant life. Jesus revealed all of this to us. We are even more aware of it in these days when a loving God, carrying out the wishes of this Good Shepherd, brings into our lives so many rich blessings.

3. Restoration

David was especially aware of the sweetness of the word, "He restoreth my soul." We can almost detect a sob in his throat when he speaks it, and almost a strange blur on the paper as he wrote it, "He restoreth my soul." Of course, if he had been talking directly of the sheep, in that particular, he would have said "the life" or "the vigor" or "the strength." By all means he would seek to bring back the fullest life and the most abundant living for the sheep, but David is talking about a human being in that split second, and one does not have to imagine very far that he is talking about himself. How tragic has been that hour of defeat and sin and shame! How tangled grew a web! How ruined the soul!

For a whole year David suffered, was in misery, knew no peace of mind or heart, struggled on, and then one day he finally went to the Good Shepherd and sobbed out what is included in the fifty-first Psalm as the sob of his soul. He repented fully and confessed his sins and poured out all of his prayer to the Good Shepherd who loved him. Then it was that the Good Shepherd restored his soul, brought back the old joys, started the music again, set the joybells going, and made him effective again as a follower of his Lord. David knew what he meant when he said, "He restoreth my soul."

How about your soul? How about mine? Not just in some

great outspoken, outbroken sin, but what about it, in the sheer weariness that comes to us either in body or mind or spirit, when we have lost something of the radiance, when we have lost the music, when we have lost something of the beauty of our Christian witness?

David said, "He restoreth my soul." Let us pray for that in our hearts! Let us plead for the kind of restoration that is available for us! It is there for the asking. The Good Shepherd wants to bring it instantly and to apply it with all of the gentleness and loving care of One who knows and cares.

4. Guide, Protector, Leader

When we come to verses 3 and 4 we are face to face with David's picture of the Shepherd as guide and guardian and protector. He is still the Shepherd, the ones he deals with are still the sheep, but this is a peculiar and delicate ministry which he performs. These sheep, who have been called away from the beaten track, from the burning sun, from the dry, hard earth to a quiet place by water, and who have been restored in body and being, are now ready to go on the way out into the highway again or across the hard places. Life for them is not resting and eating and drinking cool water.

David is trying to say that God is a Good Shepherd to him, as One who leads gently from the resting place and from the cooling waters directly into the rough going, the hard struggle, the daily grind of life itself. He is seeking always to lead us into lives of righteousness, into lives of straightness, into lives that will take a great deal of muscle and fiber and will to bring out the richer hues and to become the strong, well-developed individuals that will please the Master.

Surely David is aware of the struggles of life and the hard places of life and the righteous challenges to avoid the evil and to eliminate that which will soil and will disturb the Christian growth. He is aware also of God's great eternal righteousness that makes powerful demands on individuals who are his.

No one of us would want to be coddled and treated as

baby lambs by a cool spring with long luscious grass or any other delicacy all our lives. There is something of a lift to the assertion that the Shepherd leads us, having once prepared us in body, mind, and spirit, out into something that will challenge the very best we have.

What a challenging thought it is to have a shepherd like that, One who has purposes for our lives, who has blueprints already drawn, who has specifications written out, who has in his mind's eye a great purpose for our lives. Nothing low or vulgar or foul or little or selfish or stubborn will please him. No life that majors on missing the mark or rebellion or wilfulness can please him, so the Good Shepherd leads us directly out into the hard going and rejoices to see that the restored vigor and strength, that have come from his loving touch, provide the spark, the strength, the lift that will send us into the rough going and keep us going strong as his.

5. "I Will Fear No Evil"

When we come to verse 4, we are in the very holy of holies of the Psalms. "Yea, though I walk through the valley of the shadow of death, I will fear no evil: for thou art with me; thy rod and thy staff they comfort me."

Here we face the most precious portion of the psalm. It makes clear the confidence which has marked the career and closing hours on earth of many of God's saints. There are two words in it for our lives. First of all, a message of peace for the one who walks with the Shepherd, and a message of power for the one before whom life lies as an untrodden path. The picture he presents is the shepherd walking on ahead with his rod and his staff available for any emergency. With confidence, with assurance, with an encouraging word, he leads even through the valley of the shadow of death. The psalmist declares, "I will fear no evil: for thou art with me."

We are all acquainted by this time with the fact that the psalmist is not referring primarily to the moment of death in this lovely verse. For a Christian the moment of death is not a dark valley. It is far from being a fear-ridden moment. There are many experiences in life's way that are far more heart-rending than the moment when Jesus comes to take us home.

David is evidently describing the leading of the shepherd as he takes his sheep from one feeding place to another or from the feeding place back home to the fold late in the afternoon. Shadows have already covered the narrow gorges through which he must take them. Hostile enemies may wait to snatch one or two of the sheep. Fierce beasts are most certainly around to make the journey even more perilous. The steep mountain defile, where the sheep must go one at a time led by the shepherd, can but bring fear to the heart of all.

David declares that in life when such experiences as that are necessary he will not fear at all, because his Shepherd is present. The One who has led him into quiet places of rest and who has led him through all the hard struggles of the day's grind, the One who will gladly give his life to protect him and shield him, is present, so there is no need of fear.

The psalmist changes the figure and instead of using the third person he now says, "Thou art with me." We do not have to press this point, because it is so clear to all our hearts. Perhaps no serious sorrow or distress has come into your heart, but in many of our hearts sorrow or pain or disappointment or anguish has come like a dagger to the heart. How do we stand in hours like these? How does a person who is not a Christian and who does not have the Good Shepherd present even stand hours like that one?

David declares that the only way he is able to do it is with the assurance that his divine Shepherd is there. "Thou art with me." What a flood of memories come rolling in to bathe our souls and to lift our spirits when we realize the number of times there was need, and the eternal Good Shepherd was there!

When Paul needed him so much, Jesus said, "My grace is sufficient for thee" (2 Cor. 12: 9). Isaiah expressed it, "Thou wilt keep him in perfect peace, whose mind is stayed on thee:

because he trusteth in thee" (Isa. 26: 3). Listen to Isaiah again, "Fear not: for I have redeemed thee, I have called thee by thy name; thou art mine. When thou passest through, the waters, I will be with thee; and through the rivers, they shall not overflow thee: when thou walkest through the fire, thou shalt not be burned; neither shall the flame kindle upon thee. For I am the Lord thy God, the Holy One of Israel, thy Saviour" (Isa. 43: 1-2). Surely nothing in life is worth as much as the realization that we have the divine Shepherd as our own loving Shepherd and that each moment of the journey, whether in the open or whether in some narrow, dark shadowy place of peril or danger, we can be sure of the fact that he is present, always present.

6. The Loving Host

When we turn to verses 5 and 6, we are immediately confronted with another picture. The shepherd figure may go on through all the verses, but it seems best to think of David as changing the figure here and turning our thought on a host and applying the figure more nearly to us as individuals.

Jehovah is now pictured as a bountiful Host who entertains his guest at his own table, provides lodging in his own house, and in the very presence of the people who have been hostile to him. He devotes himself to a lavish display of love and welcome and unusual gifts that reveal his appreciation of him and his love for him.

The psalmist says, "Thou anointest my head with oil; my cup runneth over." Those two things indicate something of the lavish way in which the Shepherd provides for the joys, the luxuries, the extras of life, as well as the necessities. His guest will be happy and cheerful and glad in heart. It will be a joyous occasion all the way, because the Giver of every good and perfect gift is lavishing his best upon even a poor sinner from Bethlehem.

How wondrous it is to think of God as our Shepherd, lavishing upon us so many of the riches! Can we afford to live selfishly or live in any way unworthy of that which he expects of us? Can we waste our time or our energies or our influence? Can we soil our hands or our tongues or our faces or our souls?

Can we give any kind of occasion for stumbling to someone along the way when we are the guests of the King, yea, even the guests of the Good Shepherd and about his table we are feeding? On his bounties we are living, in his favor and bathed in his smile we are enjoying life. The psalmist would have us bow in humble gratitude as we realize the wonders connected with that gift of God.

The psalmist begins a line that has most of our minds guessing, because we are hardly prepared for the vivid way he describes the Good Shepherd's care of us in calling to his side two lovely, young helpers who are assigned to us as individuals. One of them is named "good," the other is named *hesedh* or "loving-kindness."

These two young men seemingly are the Shepherd's choicest helpers. They are prepared in every way. They are qualified beyond any question. Now they are taken away from whatever they were doing and assigned the task of walking close to our heels, day and night, not to spy on us, but to protect us, to help carry out the will and wishes of the Good Shepherd, to provide all of these bounties, to reveal all of these graces, to give to us all that God has in mind that we shall enjoy. Surely, again and again, we will bow in gratitude as we think of his provision.

7. A Home at the End of the Journey

When we come to the closing line it is almost too much for our poor minds. We are assured that there is to be a home at the end of the journey and that we are to be invited home with the Shepherd to spend all the ages of eternity.

We remember the story of Enoch and how they were walking together, Enoch and God, and after they had walked a long, long way God said, "You are nearer my house than you are yours, why not come on over and spend the rest of the time with me?" We may be sure that Enoch was thrilled to the depths of his soul. In God's great beyond he is still rejoicing in unspeakable joys as he realizes that he was chosen as a fit companion of God and that he was awarded the privilege of going home with God to spend the rest of eternity with him. We sometimes wonder if God and Enoch are still walking together.

Would it thrill you to know that your Shepherd, one day, is to invite you home to stay with him and to walk with him? You see, it was impossible to do that until Jesus became, in the fullest sense, the Good Shepherd. He said one day that he was going to give his life as an offering so that he might qualify, fully and completely, as the Good Shepherd. He did!

Calvary is the answer, and when Jesus was taken down from the cross, the debt was paid in full so that we need never remain slaves of the devil, but be free to exercise our own will and accept the Lord Jesus as our personal Saviour and let him become our Good Shepherd. Since he has given his life a ransom for us and since he loves us with such a devoted love and since he is our Shepherd, is it too much to believe that, along with David, he will lift us one day into his presence where there is a home prepared for us?

David said, "And I will dwell in the house of the Lord for ever." He is not just talking about the house at Jerusalem. Somehow, in a mysterious way, the Holy Spirit helped his spirit break over into that mystic beyond where those mansions prepared for us were for the brief moment visible, and David dared, under the leadership of the Holy Spirit, to declare that there would be a home at the end of the journey awaiting him.

Do you have a home that you can call your very own here on this earth? Perhaps you do. Many of us do not. Would it do something to your heart to be assured of the fact that one day there is a home, not made with hands, eternal in the heavens, prepared by the fingers of the Lord Jesus, ready and waiting for your coming? David gives us such an assurance. It is your privilege, it is mine, to have that assurance as our very own today.

V. How We May Have These Assurances

How may we be sure of that? The Bible gives us a perfectly good answer to that question. No amount of offering or benevolence or good living or righteous observance will make it possible. No amount of church attendance or prayers or godly behavior will have a thing to do with it. Not even church membership and baptism can affect it in the least.

How, then, can one be sure that he has the Good Shepherd as his very own and that he can have these blessings during this life and the eternal gifts on the other shore? Jesus puts it fully on the basis of simple faith in him. He makes it clear that when one trusts him, he is instantly saved. There is involved in trusting, first of all, the element of belief. He is God's Son, he died to make atonement for our sins. He wants to save us. We believe that.

Second there is trust. We commit ourselves to him, completely, unreservedly, and let him have our hearts, our lives. When we have done this, we are saved just as the thief on the cross was saved, just as the Philippian jailer was saved, just as the eunuch on the road to Ethiopia was saved.

Following the moment of actual salvation we are impelled by an inner urge to confess him as Saviour and Lord and let all peoples know that we belong to him. This is a public profession.

The fourth step involved in it all is the step that we call "obedience." If we are his, then we will want to please him.

He would want us, first, to confess him and then to obey him in baptism and in church membership. All through our lives we will give of our means and our lives and our talents, and we will bear witness to his saving power wherever we go.

When that is done, any one of us, at any spot on the globe, can claim him as our Saviour and our Good Shepherd, and we may be sure that not only through life will he guide us and lead us, but he will prepare that home for us at the end of the journey and make possible our eternal entrance into what he delightfully calls, "my Father's house."

How grateful we are to David for this presentation of this

remarkable picture of the Good Shepherd! Jesus came to make it more complete, to apply it definitely to himself, and to add the idea that he would die to make atonement for the sins of the world so that in the fullest sense he could become the Good Shepherd that would bring life and immortality and eternal joys to these to whom he ministered while on earth.

Thank God for the security, for the simplicity, for the beauty of a faith in him, for the quiet trust in the Lord Jesus, who as our Good Shepherd brings serenity of soul, the like of which no one else in the world can ever know except one who has trusted Christ.

CHAPTER IV

THE HOLY SCRIPTURES

WHEN WE ATTEMPT to find what the psalmist thought of God's holy Word, we are immediately in contact with so many different passages that we have difficulty in deciding which of them we can use. It is good to know that the psalmist, who had very little of what we call the Bible at his fingertips, had such a glorious conception of the value of these words from God's lips.

The psalmist probably had access to the books of Moses and perhaps a few of the historical books. The later psalmists had access to some of the messages of the prophets. In the main, however, the psalmist's Bible was rather small, and to those of us who look upon the New Testament with such reverence and appreciation, there might be a tendency to think of his Bible as of rather small value.

Let us look, however, through the book of Psalms and catch something of the spirit which is in evidence as we hear the poet describe the place the Scriptures ought to have in a life and their value for everyone who seeks to live a godly life.

These men were conscious of the fact that a godly life was impossible without an understanding of God's will for that life, and the best way to know God's will for a soul is to become acquainted with his Word and think on it continually. We shall look into three of the psalms for the appraisal which the psalmist places on God's Book (Psalms 1, 19, and 119).

I. THE LAW IN THE EYES OF THE GODLY MAN (PSALM 1)

But his delight is in the law of the Lord; and in his law doth he meditate day and night. And he shall be like a tree planted by the rivers of water, that bringeth forth his fruit in his season; his leaf also shall not wither; and whatsoever he doeth shall prosper.—Psalm 1: 2-3.

In the opening part of the first Psalm we are introduced immediately to one who is considered God's man. He is

49

worthy in every particular. He is well above the average in conduct, in behavior, in attitudes, in devotion to God. He has put up certain definite refusals in his life and has been remarkably powerful in staying from places where his soul would be soiled. He refuses to walk in the disposition cherished by the ungodly. He refuses to associate with the vicious life of sinners. He has no delight whatever in the society of those who scoff at religion. We watch him as he walks triumphantly on through life without a single glance in the direction of these who would lead him astray.

When asked to explain the secret of his life, the psalmist tells us that his heart and interest and affections are somewhere else. He is in love with the One who exerts a stronger influence over him. As he walks life's way he has no thought whatever of blunting the keen, sharp edge of his soul by unholy associations and hurtful atmospheres. He thinks too much of his soul to let it be soiled by slurs and cynical remarks of cynics.

1. He Delights in the Law

We still inquire of the psalmist the real secret. We know that there is something beyond this, and so he tells us in a very simple sentence, "His delight is in the law [Torah] of the Lord." There is nothing in the world that he enjoys more than the teaching of God. It is sweet to his taste, it is soothing, it is nourishing, it is toothsome and much to be desired. It has become the rule of his life. He literally absorbs himself in the kind of meditation, day and night, on God's Word that opens its hidden meaning to him. He continually keeps himself busy at this task, which to him is a delightful one, of searching and meditating upon the teaching of God.

We are apt to think in terms of the word "law" as being either a stern discipline suggested for us, or else we are apt to think of it technically as being the Pentateuch. The psalmist thinks of it in a much wider way than this. The word, out of which our noun comes, is the verb *yarah*, "to teach," and the law of God, as the psalmist describes it here, is that which comes from the brain and heart and mouth of the eternal Father in heaven. It is his Word to men's hearts. He knows what men need. He knows the tonic, the nourishment, the strength-giving quality, the guidance, the sustaining lift, the word of warning, and anything else that his creature needs for the fullest life imaginable.

So the psalmist tells us that this particular man, who has reached such eminence as a powerful man of God, has revealed his secret. He loves and enjoys and feasts upon and meditates upon that which has come from God's heart for his mind and heart. He has learned to enjoy the taste of it. He is greatly blessed by the soul-satisfying nourishment that comes. He recognizes it as food for his hungry soul. It nourishes, quickens, enriches, restores, freshens, and broadens his capacities.

In the law of the Lord, God's man finds what God has to say to him. It is God's love letter to him. It is God's word of genuine counsel. He finds in it those qualities that are most needed in becoming victorious along the way. It is no irksome restriction of his liberty, but he has learned to love the Word of God so much that he delights in the constant study of its rich messages. He finds that his truest happiness comes in learning and feasting upon the revealed will of God.

2. What the Law Does in the Heart

The psalmist further recommends the reading and studying of God's holy Word by describing what happens in the life of this man who is habitually engaged in the study of the will of God. He declares that he is like a tree firmly planted by the water courses and that as a result of his being firmly planted, he not only stands solidly and securely against any storm that may come, but he is maintained by the supplies of grace drawn from constant communion with God through this divine revelation. He is ever fresh and renewed and alive so that the stately growth, the evergreen foliage, the much-to-be-desired fruit come naturally and regularly as an added blessing, because of his grip on these eternal verities.

The figure used here is so engaging that it is a great challenge to us to begin taking this spiritual vitamin that will
do all of that for us. You have seen a person's eyes light up
with interest and desire when someone describes a new vitamin that renews life and vigor and freshness and beauty.
Eagerly he asks for the name of that life-giving vitamin.

We can imagine that the author of this psalm must have
been confronted by many who asked him to help them secure
this guaranteed remedy that could produce such changes in
body and face and mind and heart and give strength that
would please not only men, but be exceptionally pleasing to
the Heavenly Father.

Thus the author of the first Psalm describes for us the picture of the one whose roots were continually feeding on the
eternal fountains that produced fruit in due season. All of
the distresses and sorrows and misfortunes that came upon
him caused this man of God to dig deeper to find and enjoy
the inexhaustible supply of God's life-giving resources. If
you are drawing daily from that fountain that produces such
attractive and desirable results, your life will be a rich life
that will please our Creator and lead others to seek him.

Delitzsch has this comment: "That which a brook full of
water is to the tree that is planted close beside it, the word of
God is to the man who devotes himself to it; it makes him,
according to his calling in life, ever fruitful in seasonable
good works, it keeps him vigorous both inwardly and outwardly; and everything that such an one undertakes he
brings to a successful issue, for the strength of the word and
of the blessing of God is in all that he does." (*Commentary
on the Psalms,* pp. 13-14.)

If you would like to be sure that everything you do will
result in your being able to carry through to a successful con-
clusion your aims and purposes, then by all means let God's
holy Word be your portion day and night. As the water
taken in by the roots of the tree becomes a part of the sap
which permeates to the extreme end of every twig and leaf,
so let the Word of God permeate your whole personality.
The inevitable result will be a fruitful life.

II. The Beauty and Power of the Law (Psalm 19)

The law of the Lord is perfect, converting the soul: the testimony of the Lord is sure, making wise the simple. . . . Moreover by them is thy servant warned: and in keeping of them there is great reward.—Psalm 19: 7, 11.

In this poem the author pictures with vividness the revelation of God in nature, in the second division the moral beauty and power of Jehovah's law in its manifold aspects, and in the closing part of the chapter he is driven to a prayer for pardon and for preservation. Verses 1—6 give us this revelation of God in nature, and we are confronted with the majesty and wonder and glory of God. Beginning with verse 7 we are face to face with the power of the Word as it reveals something of Jehovah's will and quickens man's moral nature so that he is constantly drawn to God and is strengthened in every area of his being to become a man after God's own heart.

Again let us remember that the word "law" as found in this psalm denotes more than the first five books of Moses and includes all of God's sayings and God's messages to men. It certainly includes all of the books of the Bible that were then in his hands and would include today all of the books of the New Testament.

The psalmist has much to say about the law and uses many different words for it. He uses different adjectives to describe it. For instance, it is *perfect, sure, right, pure, clean, true, righteous,* and it is so wondrous in its effect upon human beings that its messages have the answer for all men's questions and govern all his ways and meet perfectly all his needs. That alone would cause us to turn immediately to it in the hope that we might gain something of that power for ourselves. He declares that the moral nature is quickened and educated so that a man is much more than an ordinary man, mentally, physically, and spiritually. It does something for the moral fiber of the individual which is transmitted into all of the areas of the life until in every way he is improved so that it is noticeable by men and by the divine eye.

We are rejoiced to know that the law is declared to have power in restoring the soul. It can actually build up the kind of moral tissue that has been broken down and destroyed. When a man has lost his strength and his nerve, he comes to the law and finds the kind of blessing that will restore all of it and set him on his feet to go again. This restoring quality comes to refresh and invigorate the man just as food would to a hungry person or as exceptional comfort would to one whose heart has been broken.

The psalmist goes a step further to say that this revelation of God to man is not variable or uncertain, but always dependable and always available, and in each instance will do for the individual what his heart needs. His next word declares that it makes the heart glad with the joy of moral satisfaction. How that appeals to our heart! Who among us would not like to have his heart made glad, to find precisely the remedy that provides an elixir that will change the atmosphere of the heart so that the joybells can ring? The psalmist has found it.

The author of this psalm then declares that the law of God is clean or pure. That is quite a contrast when we lay it alongside of the kind of immoralities of the pagans. Just as Jehovah is clean, so any word that has come from his mouth is clean and pure, and just as he stands fast forever so any word that he speaks will be true and eternally dependable to the very end of time.

These are examples of what the psalmist has to say about God's Word in this psalm. The psalmist declares that it will make the simple one wise. When we meditate upon the Scriptures, there is a poise and a balance and a peculiar wisdom that instinctively becomes ours. There is a restoration of the inner juices that comes as a definite result of feasting upon it, and one who has been afflicted or tired or disturbed or heartsick, finds after quiet meditation on the Scriptures that which will bring new life and new strength to the heart.

The poet goes on to say that God's law is a greater treasure than the finest gold and the most precious silver, and then, to cap it all off, he declares that it brings life a sweetness that is more to be desired than the finest honey that can be found. We might go on with these beautiful words that the psalmist uses to describe the effect of God's Word upon the individual. Let us pause to see one more. He declares that it enlightens the eyes and makes the eye capable of seeing.

Instead of seeking something that will give us an uncanny ability to make decisions, to interpret Scriptures, or to impress others with our brilliance, the psalmist would have us go to the Scriptures and feast on them and let them come into our hearts so that a peculiar wisdom will be ours. His prescription is that we must meditate upon God's holy Word.

We have seen those who have majored on the study of God's Word. We have understood something of their keen and penetrating interpretations. We have wondered how they stood up under such loads and faced the world with such radiant faces and kept themselves so untroubled and calm in the midst of everything that swept over them. The psalmist would answer our question and declare that the kind of thinking on God's Word that he recommends will have its effect in equipping us so that every day will reveal new victories, and every experience will find a remedy ready at hand.

In another line the poet says, "Moreover by them is thy servant warned." If we found no other value in them than the power of the Scripture to flash a red light for us at many turns in the road, we would be amply repaid for all of the effort in becoming acquainted with these words from the Book. How many, many times in the life of the psalmist did he find the flash of a red signal announcing something that was to be avoided, or the approach of the tempter, announcing peril or danger, assuring him of guidance and protection, making certain his confidence and his courage, and equipping him with new reserves, the like of which he had never known.

How about that for your life and mine? Would it be good to have the Scriptures stored up in our hearts so that all through life's rugged way we could have a blessing like that available? The psalmist tells us that we may have it. It is

God's will that we shall have it, and it will be a constant reward as we keep these words of the Book.

III. GOD'S ETERNAL WORD (PSALM 119)

> *Wherewithal shall a young man cleanse his way? by taking heed thereto according to thy word. . . . Thy word have I hid in mine heart, that I might not sin against thee. . . . So shall I have wherewith to answer him that reproacheth me: for I trust in thy word. . . . For ever, O Lord, thy word is settled in heaven. . . . Unless thy law had been my delight, I should then have perished in mine affliction. . . . O how love I thy law! it is my meditation all the day. . . . Thy word is a lamp unto my feet, and a light unto my path. . . . The entrance of thy words giveth light; it giveth understanding unto the simple.*—Psalm 119: 9, 11, 42, 89, 92, 97, 105, 130.

In Psalm 119 we have the most remarkable presentation of the things that may be said concerning the law of God in all the Bible. The religious ideas of Deuteronomy are thought on and developed by some devout soul who was able to bring a spiritual interpretation of the Deuteronomic conception of the value of God's revelation to man.

It was the author's steadfast purpose to make God's law the guiding principle of his conduct, to bring all of his will and aims under God's direction, to make his whole life in accord with the perfect will of God. To do all of this he majored on God's Word. How he ever found time to do anything else is your question. Day and night he lived with it, it became the very food of his mind. He fell desperately in love with God and then just as deeply in love with God's Word and God's will for his life.

The psalm consists of 176 verses, each verse, with one or two exceptions, has something to say about God's holy Word. It is an acrostic. Each of the first eight verses begins with *Alef*, the first letter of the Hebrew alphabet. Each of the second eight verses begins with the letter *Beth*, the second letter of the Hebrew alphabet, and so on through all the Hebrew letters, making twenty-two sections in all, containing eight verses each.

We are told that St. Augustine deferred the exposition of it until he had finished the rest of the Psalter and finally approached it with great reluctance because of its difficult character and depth of meaning. Mr. Ruskin once said that this psalm had become of all the most precious to him in its overflowing passion of love for the law of God.

We can never know who wrote the psalm. Evidently the poet's heart had been sorely tried, and in the midst of God's loving discipline he had learned to trust the divine wisdom and to seek his will. In the midst of contempt and ill treatment and persecution and mocking and oppression and danger of his life he endured, pledging himself in each instance to lean more heavily upon the One who was his Lord and to feed more continuously upon the Word which was the source of all of his help. His prayer was that he might have a fuller knowledge of the law and that he might be given added strength day by day to keep it, because in his hours of cruel persecution he needed the solace of the Lord who had taught him in its pages.

We may not know whether the poet was a young man, as Delitzsch thinks, or an old man, as Ewald claims. Perhaps a better solution would be that he was a man of maturity who had suffered much and who had learned many things from bitter experience and from his leaning on God who came in answer to his call. He is reverent and full of gratitude and prayerful in his approach to God.

The most noteworthy thing about this man is that he is an enthusiastic lover of the law. Deuteronomy 6:5 had indicated that the true Israelite would fall in love with the law and with God who had given it. This author seems to have measured up to this high standard in full measure. He says, "O, how I love thy law! it is my meditation all the day." He does not regard the time spent upon study and meditation as something that is a burden, but his joy, his delight, his comfort, the subject of his meditations by day and night, the source of his faith and trust and hope in the midst of the severe troubles that plague his life.

In it all the psalmist says, "Thy word is a lamp unto my feet, and a light unto my path." We will seek to single out certain passages in the psalm that indicate his love for and appreciation of the Scriptures. Perhaps, as we hear him tell of his love for the law, we will become more appreciative of its treasures. Let us remember that when he uses the word "law," he is referring to the whole revelation of God to man. It is God teaching and whatever God has taught is the Torah which is so precious to this psalmist.

Let us begin by taking verse 9 and see something of the way the psalmist gets right into the middle of a problem that is thoroughly alive in our world today. He asks the question "Wherewithal shall a young man cleanse his way?" and then proceeds immediately to answer it in these words, "By taking heed thereto according to thy word."

It is interesting to know that the psalmist is greatly concerned about the young men of his day. He knows perfectly well that there will be temptations, there will be needs. He knows that in the midst of a world such as his and with creatures such as his companions were that a young man of his acquaintance would need the help of God's Word to make it possible for him to cleanse his way and, of course, in order to cleanse his way he would need to cleanse his heart first of all. It is a difficult thing to make a way clean, and it is even more difficult to make the heart clean or pure.

The psalmist was concerned that this young man be clean from the stain of sin and that he begin by hiding the Word in his heart that he might be strong in the hour of temptation. He realizes that in the midst of all of his difficulties God has not left us without instruction and without direction and without the assurance of his help in all the trials of life. He would not leave a young man to struggle on, becoming soiled at each turn in the road. It is God's thoughtful way of providing for him that has brought the Scriptures into being, and the author of this psalm would have us realize that, no matter how careful we are in trying to regulate our own life, we need more than anything else God's Word to make for great living.

In our day we must be genuine Christians and trust the Lord Jesus Christ, first for forgiveness for past sins and then for strength for the future to walk in a new life and to have victory as we walk. The psalmist tells us that the Word of God will direct us in each of these steps and provide the direction whereby we can find help from the Saviour who alone can make victory possible.

The psalmist says, "Thy word have I hid in mine heart, that I might not sin against thee." The word "hide" is perhaps best translated, *laid up* or *stored up, treasured in my heart as a safeguard against sin.*

It is quite easy to think of sin as being of little moment and probably not amounting to much in our life, but the psalmist declares that the way he has prepared himself to meet and to conquer sin is to store up the Word of God in his heart and to have it as a powerful safeguard as he walks the way. It is a strong preventive against the contagion of sin. It is a serum that makes a man immune to the danger of turning aside. It is a keen observation that the psalmist makes when he declares that this Word in his heart is going to make the going easier for him and make victories more certain for him as he carries on.

What about your provision for the journey ahead? Do you have stored up in your heart that which will provide protection and guidance and victory? The psalmist would urge you, whatever else you carry with you on a journey, to have as your precious possession the Word of God stored away where it is instantly available for any use.

You will remember that the author of Psalm 19 said, "By means of it thy servant is warned." There we saw the red lights flashing to warn. Here we see the actual protection provided deep in the heart of one who encounters the tempter and who suffers the indignities of those who would cause trouble and distress and defeat. Surely we would like to be prepared for the emergencies ahead. The psalmist declares for us that we can depend upon the Word of God to be ours in the moment of need.

In verse 18 we hear a rather unusual prayer when the psalmist prays, "Lord, please uncover my eyes that I may behold wondrous things." In the Word of God there are many things that are difficult for the human understanding. As a matter of fact we go on without ever knowing the full meaning of many of these choice passages, until we have God withdraw the covering of natural shortsightedness from our eyes so that we can see. The psalmist cheers our hearts when he tells us, by his own example, that God is waiting to hear and to withdraw the covering from our eyes so that we shall be able to discern the mysteries of divine revelation. God delights to hear a prayer like this. The psalmist has done us a real service in assuring us that this is possible for us.

The prayer in verse 33 is another choice reminder that we can learn a good deal if we are willing to pray for it. The poet wants, in this prayer, instruction and guidance, because he wants to escape the false ways of selfishness. He wants to be in the fullest sense one of God's chosen to whom God can speak and on whom God can depend. He realizes that the way this will be brought about is by means of the statutes or the commandments of God which are to be taught him when his prayer is answered by the loving Father.

In verse 42 the psalmist is praying that he may have grace to enable him to make a true and joyous confession of his faith in God, and that he may have such a personal experience of God's loving-kindness manifested in his deliverance that he will be strong and equipped to reply to those who taunt him and ridicule him. He wants to be able to bring a conclusive and convincing answer to them when they laugh at him for worshiping a God who is unable to do anything for him.

One of the greatest things God's Word can do for us is to prepare us to be effective in giving an answer not only to those who revile us and make fun of us, but to all those who might be unacquainted with the wonders of God's grace and loving-kindness. Surely a prayer like this one is a worthy one for any Christian. We may well join him in that prayer.

In verses 66, 71, and 72 we find the psalmist declaring that his afflictions have given him the privilege of understanding the true meaning of God's Word. He has not only had time to read and think, but he has found vistas that were otherwise closed to him. He now knows that God's hand is sometimes heavy upon us in order to bring about the state of mind that will allow the holy Word to come in and do its work. The psalmist is grateful for his afflictions because of this value that has come to him.

In verse 89 he declares, "For ever, O Lord thy word is settled in heaven." We are delighted that he has taken this leap in describing that the Word of God not only has heaven as its standing place, but that the very qualities of heaven are within it and that it is eternal in its existence. It can never be changed. It embraces all of the needs of men. It applies to all of the problems of men. It has been his support in hours of distress. It will continue to be an eternal help for any who call upon him.

In verse 92 the author of this psalm refers to his afflictions again and declares that, "Unless thy law had been my delights, I should then have perished in mine affliction." He is aware of the tremendous bit of refreshment that came to him during his illness by reading and thinking of God's Word.

The psalmist attributes the healing touch to this Word of God. How many others could give a testimony like this if they could but realize how much God's Word has meant in hours of distress and illness and need? What a lift it gives and how the balances may be shifted by means of the lift which the holy Word, God's message, brings to their hearts!

In verse 97, 98, 99, and 100 the psalmist breaks forth with a word that is perfectly beautiful. He says, "O how love I thy law! It is my meditation all the day. Thou through thy commandments hast made me wiser than mine enemies: for they are ever with me. I have more understanding than all my teachers: for thy testimonies are my meditation. I understand more than the ancients, because I keep thy precepts."

The author is not only shouting aloud his love for the law, but in addition he declares that these teachers of his and the older men of the community, who were supposed to be so wise, are behind him now in actual knowledge of God's will for a human life, because in the crucible of suffering he has learned much that they have yet to learn as they go forward in their training. It may be that there is a reference here to the fact that some of the teachers, as well as the elders, were not as close to the Lord as they might be for a fuller revelation of his will for their lives. The law, in other words, is the one source of instruction that is a veritable fountain of wisdom and prudence and discernment.

The psalmist has learned from God's Word that which could never be learned from any other source. It is not difficult for us to accept this, because we know perfectly well that some of our saints who have suffered most and who have prayed most fervently and who have lived with God's holy Word have come out of that crucible with new understanding of the richer things of God. How wise we could be if we would only go to God's Book for the true wisdom!

In verse 105 the psalmist says, "Thy word is a lamp unto my feet, and a light unto my path." He is thoroughly aware of the value of God's law as the guide of life. He now says this guide is a lamp to guide him safely in the midst of the worst perils of the pathway. It may be dark, it may be slippery, there may be dangerous ravines along the way, other dangers may lurk, but the Word of God will be for him a continual lamp unto his feet and a light to his path.

That lamp or that torch is to the author the most precious bit of equipment that he takes on his hazardous journey through life. He would urge parents who send their sons and daughters out into a world with so many traps and unknown forks in the road, with so many difficulties, to see that these youngsters have this light, this torch, this lamp. If parents are not going to do much about it, our young people should equip themselves completely for life's journey, knowing full well that God's Word will always be the one indispensable lamp for their feet.

In verse 111 the psalmist says, "Thy testimonies have I taken as an heritage for ever: for they are the rejoicing of my heart." He is describing his one precious treasure that is an inheritance more valuable than all others. If enemies are to attack him and take from him all other possessions, his claim is that this one will be kept. Even if it is not in book form it will be his, for it has been transferred from the pages of the book to the heart.

If you will note, the Psalms make no reference anywhere to reading at night, and yet the psalmist declared that the night watches are the time that they do most of their work on the law of God. The mind has written on it the words of this inheritance and no matter what robbers or bandits may do, this inheritance is to be his forever. He values it and will delight to keep it.

In verse 130 the writer says, "The entrance of thy words giveth light; it giveth understanding unto the simple." The greatest desire of the psalmist seems to be that he may have light. He prays that he may have God's Word as life-giving food, even though there are those about him who hate him and persecute him severely and delight to take away from him any possession that is considered valuable. He comes up with the statement that when God's Word enters his mind light immediately breaks forth, because there is understanding and when understanding comes, light is present. He is delighted to know that it is God himself who uncovers the mind and unravels the mysteries of his Word to everyone who seeks, to everyone who prays for revelation and light and knowledge.

Again, how foolish we are to remain engrossed in anything else in life's way, however important, when God's Word is literally waiting to bring light and knowledge and understanding and when God, who is back of those words, is desirous of revealing the hidden meaning not only of the actual words, but of his will that is available for all men who would walk the way perfectly.

In verse 140 the author says, "Thy word is very pure: therefore thy servant loveth it." Again he is opening a new facet and revealing a new thought concerning the Word of God. It is tried or refined as pure gold. There is absolutely no dross in it, there is nothing at all that slightly resembles a blemish; being fire-tested, it is the best metal. It is because of this that the psalmist is in love with it and treasures it among his rare treasures.

In verse 165 the psalmist says, "Great peace have they that love thy law: and they have no occasion of stumbling" (ASV). It is because this man loves God's law and knows God's law and has it deep in his mind and heart that he has great peace. It is an inward peace, even in the midst of outward persecution. It is the kind of peace which one enjoys amid the turmoil and strife and confusion that is round about, and when one is equipped with this law or this Word of God, he will be guided in his steps so that he will not stumble. God looks after one who is filled with and equipped with his holy Word. A great deal of it becomes intelligible to him. Many of its treasured passages are not intelligible except in the moment when the need presents itself and the Holy Spirit, in his own way, brings that passage before him and interprets its full meaning for him.

In all of the study of God's will let us never lose sight of the fact that the Holy Spirit is our teacher, that he is the interpreter, that he takes truth that, without his help, would be just a group of words, and breathes into it the full meaning that is instantly understandable to one who is in touch with him.

As we turn from the study of this chapter, may each of us go into a quiet place with God and on bended knee promise him that we will take his holy Word and make it the lamp of our feet and the light for our path. We need just what the psalmist found. We perhaps need it more than he did. Will you join me in a diligent search for the truths that are worth more than all else in life put together?

Chapter V

HOW DEAL WITH SIN

IN ALL AGES men have wrestled with the problem of sin. Some have struggled and sought a remedy and then have collapsed in despair. Others have invented ways of meeting and dealing with it. The Bible is everywhere aware of the seriousness of the problem, and we are constantly brought back to God, who alone can do something about this tragic situation. The book of Psalms gives us the best thinking of men on this matter.

In learning to deal with sin, we turn immediately to the fifty-first Psalm and seek to find the way David arrived at the solution. If we watch him in his soul-struggle and see how he fought and wrestled and writhed without a victory and then watch him as he realizes that the problem has no human solution, we will be disturbed in heart. As we continue listening to his sobs and his confessions, as we watch his hot tears, as we listen to his fears of eternal punishment and banishment from God's face and presence, we are frightened even more. We sense that he recognizes the fact that he is guilty of sins that put him beyond any remedy heretofore provided.

When David takes inventory and realizes that even though he is a king and has multitudes of bulls and goats and wealth beyond computation, he is still brought face to face with the fact that all of these worldly treasures, all of these man-made remedies, fail in the crucial moment when sin is to be dealt with. The bite of the serpent has produced a malady that defies all human help.

The poor sinner lies trembling and helpless in the trap that has already been sprung. He realizes that no human physician, that no strong arm of friend or foe, can release him from the grip of sin's chains. He has committed an act that lays him in the dust before God. All the joy has flown from his mind and heart. Unbearable pains afflict him night and day.

The stroke of God's punishing hand is felt through the

long night watches. He realizes that God has been offended and that something must be done to bring about a reconciliation, as well as a healing process. Nathan has come with his devastating accusation and his terrific charge of murder and adultery. The child of Bathsheba has been smitten with a fatal disease and has just passed away.

After these soul-shaking experiences, we find the blunt charge, the repentance, the pardon, the punishment, and the soul-struggle that reveal to us the way a sin-stricken soul finds its way back to God, to forgiveness, to cleansing and restoration, and to effectiveness throughout the entire life.

One sometimes wonders how David became such a spiritual giant and produced such eternally helpful psalms. Those of us who have sought earnestly for the answer to this question have found it in the words which have become precious to all Bible lovers recorded for us in the fifty-first and the thirty-second Psalms.

As we study Psalm 51, let us seek to lose sight of the fact that we are trying to understand a beautiful poem, a treatise on theology, a handbook for soul-winners, an unforgettable treatise on the approach of a soul to God, and let us turn ourselves loose to get hold of the feeling that breathes through these words.

Let us hope and pray that for our own hearts and for those who come to us for guidance, we may understand something of guilt and forgiveness and the undying love of God for sin-sick and sin-bound souls. We will find much help for ourselves and much for those who are about us when we study this vivid portrayal of the emotions that succeed one another in the penitent heart.

We will hear the man of God as he pictures clearly for us the nature and consequences of sin in a human being. We will hear him as he pours out his fervent prayer for complete restoration in every area of his body, mind, and spirit. We will be greatly blessed in seeing with him his idea of the way out of the tragic trap into which he has cast himself. A clear understanding of these matters will make us infinitely better prepared to think and act and teach others.

I. LORD, FORGIVE (PSALM 51: 1–2)

Have mercy upon me, O God, according to thy loving-kindness: according unto the multitude of thy tender mercies blot out my transgressions. Wash me thoroughly from mine iniquity, and cleanse me from my sin. For I acknowledge my transgressions: and my sin is ever before me. . . . Purge me with hyssop, and I shall be clean: wash me, and I shall be whiter than snow. Make me to hear joy and gladness; that the bones which thou hast broken may rejoice. Hide thy face from my sins, and blot out all mine iniquities. Create in me a clean heart, O God; and renew a right spirit within me. Cast me not away from thy presence; and take not thy holy spirit from me. Restore unto me the joy of thy salvation; and uphold me with thy free spirit. Then will I teach transgressors thy ways: and sinners shall be converted unto thee. . . . And my mouth shall shew forth thy praise.—Psalm 51: 1–3, 7–13, 15.

In verses 1 and 2 David makes reference to a remedy for man's greatest need. He understands that nothing in the world will ever bring peace to his soul or light to his eye or joy to his heart until he has felt the full forgiveness of God. Mercy is his one plea. He could not say "my God." A guilty soul who dreads justice and longs for mercy turns imploringly to God with the urgent call to be fully pardoned, completely forgiven. He gives expression to the fact that God alone is the source of mercy and forgiveness. He knows God well enough to be able to trust him completely for this pardon.

No person is ever thoroughly able to pray for pardon and forgiveness until he has recognized the fact that nothing can be done by any human being to bring about the desired help in his heart. It seems that David was most perfectly prepared by coming with a broken and a contrite heart and praying with all the fervor of his soul that God might do something about it. Without hesitation he spreads his sins before God. Each one of those sins is black and ugly.

In order to present the picture fully so that no area of his black life might be forgotten, David uses all three words for sin, each of them representing a facet in the full picture. The word *pesha* represents the picture of a rebellious soul, guilty of transgressing wilfully the law of God. There has been in David's heart this particular break with God that is represented by wilful transgression.

The second word is *awon*. This word is usually translated "iniquity." It has the root meaning of depravity or a state of crookedness. The more delicate strands of heart and character have been twisted until the heart is out of tune with and out of touch with God.

The third word is *hatah*. This word is usually translated "sin." The root idea is missing the aim or the mark. The whole tenor of his life has been in the wrong direction since he disturbed the sight so completely that he would necessarily miss the mark. What a pity it is when a life has veered from the straight aim and has become a miserable miss!

David realized that all three of these angles of sin entered into the full picture of his sin-life. He knew that he had rebelliously taken things into his own hand and gone his own way and broken God's commands. He knew that as a result of this his life had been twisted and warped and made an ugly thing, that try as he might, he could never make it right again.

David understood, too, that God had had a marvelous purpose for him and had written out the set of specifications for his life and had prepared blueprints that could be fulfilled only by one whose aim was true. He realized, as he looked at his life, how hopelessly he had missed the aim and how his life now was off the beam and off the line and that since he could never change the sight on the rifle, his whole life would end up in a wreck, unless he could be brought back by the creative touch of God and started on the right track again.

How wonderful it is to follow David's clear reasoning as he pictures sin in his own life! Is that true in the life of someone you know? Could it be true in your life? David, who wrote this immortal poem three thousand years ago, would drive home to your mind and to your heart something of the tragic sense of failure and rebellion and the deplorable picture of one who has been all messed up by sin's power in his life. Do you wonder then that he begged for forgiveness?

David looked back to the days on the hills about Bethlehem and realized something of God's goodness and something of God's plan and purpose for his life. He sensed something of the investment that his mother and father had made in him and something of Samuel's faith in him as he anointed him with the oil of consecration. He remembered that, in some strange way, as a result of that never-to-be-forgotten experience, the Spirit of God had come upon him and in all of it his mind grasped the thought that God, through his purpose and plan and ideal for his life, had projected a divinely planned life. Now as he looks upon the picture he is aware of the utter failure and also aware of God's heartbreak. The psalmist is crushed as he looks into the true picture of the future and realizes that without God failure, complete and final, must be the portion to be expected.

How about facing up honestly to all of that in your life! How about helping young lives see the tragic situation when sin takes over in human lives! How about pausing long enough here to let everyone in the class and everyone in your family meditate on the serious nature of dealing lightly with God's purpose for a life! Surely David was dealing here with something that is tremendously up-to-the-minute for your thinking and mine. No one of us can claim to be wholly exempt from this situation. God would have us face honestly his challenge and then come as David did on our knees begging forgiveness and pardon. We are sure that God will hear and answer even as he heard and answered David.

David uses three words to indicate something of the inner longing of his heart when he begs God to blot out the record of his rebellion, to wash his defiled and unclean heart, to cleanse him so that he will be clean enough for the very eyes of God. He is sick of sin. He wants a miracle to be performed. He is not willing to ask for the kind of entrance that will merely allow him to sit in a corner still defiled and unclean and unforgiven. He is going all the way in begging God for a complete and thorough work in his soul.

Sin is a heavy burden that David would like to have God take from his shoulders. It is a deep-lying pollution that only God can scrub from the tissues of his heart. It is a cruel bondage that he begs God to remove from him. It is a contaminated, soiled robe that must be made clean. It is a blotched record that must be erased. It is a fatal disease that has already found its way to the deeper places of his heart that must be counteracted by God's remedy. Surely David is on the right track when he brings all of this to God with an urgent plea that God will handle it all.

II. SINCERE CONFESSION (PSALM 51: 3–5)

The second part of David's prayer is a full confession of his own guilt. He deliberately goes out of his way to take all the blame on himself. He makes reference to the fact that he was born in sin. We all recognize that truth. David was even more conscious of it perhaps than any of us, but he was not in any sense seeking to take any of the blame off himself. He seems to present that statement with the definite assurance that he was not blaming his mother or father or any one connected with his life.

Not even Bathsheba is blamed as David talks with God. Perhaps she was a part of the picture, so far as blame is concerned, but David in this moment of passionate prayer claims every single bit of the guilt. He does not blame a generation that has lowered standards. He does not blame circumstances that threw the two of them together. He does not blame any person who gave him the wrong line somewhere back in his life.

As fully and as completely as it is possible for one to do, David reached out, put his long arms around the entire bundle of guilt, and lifted it all to his own head and laid it there and said: "God, this is my portion. I am guilty. I am confessing fully all the guilt."

In this generation it is easy for us to get quite a distance from that point as we deal with sin. David recognized that nothing in the world could bring about the victory that he was seeking until confession brought forth from his heart and mind every single bit of this sin so that those bits could be laid before God in their ugliness and in their vile fulness. Nothing could be held back. It was an absolute confession without any sort of excuse, without any extenuating circumstances, without any attempt to rationalize or leave himself the slightest bit of ground on which to stand.

Confession is just as essential as repentance. In the first section repentance has been completely pictured. There is no question in anybody's mind about David's willingness to repent fully and completely. We are just as sure that this second step of confession is as complete and as thorough.

When we place the two together we have made a long stride toward complete forgiveness and a life destined to be after God's own heart. Nathan had said, "Thou art the man." David says to God: "I am the man. Please take me in this state of sin and failure and deal with me as one whose heart is fully and completely open before the throne of God."

It is thrilling to see the guilty sinner cast himself wholly upon the mercy of God. He has no other plea. We watch the grand adventure of a man who is king, and yet is a vile sinner, throw himself impetuously upon the mercy of divine goodness. He is humble as one could be and yet he is strangely daring in making such big drafts on the infinite resources of God's love.

Not once does David think that it will be possible to call for slight gifts from God's mercy as a result of ceremonial deeds or gifts. There is no thought in his mind that salvation can be purchased by any ritualistic behavior or by animal sacrifice. No poultice of ritual will be placed upon the cancer of sin in the hope that healing may come. There is a desperate sense of need that makes him willing to offer all of the sacrifices at his disposal, but he is sure that the kind of God he knows and loves will call for something other than these outward and material efforts at restoration.

III. Make Me Clean (Psalm 51: 7–9)

In verses 7–9 David begs for the privilege of the kind of cleansing touch that would make him fit for the divine presence. It is strange to find one so meticulous in his desires that he will go to the last length to be able to come into God's presence wholly without stain or odor or undesirable marks of any kind.

David wants to be fit for that sacred place. He is unwilling to have God welcome him and then be ashamed of him because of his sins. He prays for the touch that will make him clean and pure and sweet as he comes close up to God. There is a great hope in his heart that God will bring him back to moral decency and then continue the full cleansing so that the divine eye can see purity of life. Outward respectability is not worth much in David's thinking. He wants his inner spiritual instincts to be holy and righteous.

We occasionally refer to the fact that we have to live with ourselves, and in order to be truly happy we must be clean so that under no circumstances we need be ashamed of ourselves. We call upon ourselves to be careful in the presence of others lest we offend by any kind of unpleasant impression. David is concerned that his body and mind and heart shall be completely cleansed to the place where God will not be offended. His sins, that are now so ugly in his sight, must be put so far away that God will not have to look on them. He wants them blotted out completely.

It is not for pardon alone that David pleads, but for the kind of purity that will admit him to his old place in God's plan for his life. He wants the spontaneous joyfulness of soul to be evident as he faces others about him.

Is it asking too much to expect you or me to pray this part of David's prayer? Should we be content with sinful hearts and soiled hands and impure minds and hearts that are out of tune? Should we seek to make ourselves believe that God can be pleased with us simply because we have adopted the ritual or become members of his church or been baptized into his fellowship without the kind of cleansing that David demands for himself? It seems to those of us who have caught something of the spirit of David that he was delving into depths here that are rare areas.

Perhaps our people can sense something of the ugliness of sin and become sensitive to the fact that God must be sorely displeased with us. Perhaps we can pray this prayer of the psalmist and come to God for the kind of cleansing that will make us fully and completely acceptable, even in his holy presence.

If we could only impress our children and our family group with the sacredness of God's presence! We are careful to ask the children, even as we demand of ourselves, that clean hands and clean linen and clean faces be evidenced when friends come into the home or when we go into their homes. Would it be a good move for us in our families to consider the sacred responsibility of carefulness in this one matter of being clean so that God can be pleased with us?

David is stepping on sacred ground when he talks with God like this. Surely we need to face him with this same prayer. Perhaps we have been Christians a good while, perhaps we claim to be reasonably good Christians. Are we content with a lower standard than is expressed in this simple prayer of the great sinner, David?

Not only does David want his heart and his life to be cleansed, but he wants God to come and sprinkle with hyssop the newly cleansed body and mind and heart so that everyone will know that God's approval is upon him. Surely it is not going too far in saying that David wanted the divine stamp of approval upon himself. He was facing Nathan, the prophet, and the godly men and women who made up the spiritual colony of Jerusalem. He was facing Bathsheba, who was to be his wife through the years and the mother of his son, Solomon. He was facing the people of his kingdom. His earnest plea is not only that his heart and body be cleansed, but that the priestly stamp of approval be placed upon his forehead indicating that he is now right with God after forgiveness and pardon and cleansing.

IV. Longing for Soul Music (Psalm 51: 10–12)

David's next earnest plea is that joy and gladness come to
live with him again. We need to read Psalm 32 to understand
something of the misery that David had endured during that
year. We need to take a leaf out of our own book to visualize
perhaps the lack of joy that David experienced.

Like a little child begging a father, David pleads that the
music which had gone out of his life might begin again. He
longs for the ringing of the bells in his soul. He wants to
hear the joybells again. He knows perfectly well that the
choirs and the choral groups and the priests and the members
of the religious circle cannot produce that joy in his soul. He
understands that the bells can never ring until this sin has
been removed, but he does believe that God, who pardons
and forgives, can cleanse and that when the last stroke of
cleansing has been made the music will break out again.

Perhaps we might pause for a moment in the discussion
to ask each of us to look into our own hearts. No one of us
would want to be a party to declaring that the good old days
were the only days. We could, however, profitably face the
time in our lives when there was more music of the divine
quality in our souls. Was there a time somewhere when God
was more real to you? Was there a time when his Word was
more precious, when his presence was more actual? Has
something happened in your life to drive the music out?
Have you been miserable?

David declares the true way to joy and gladness and rejoicing. He makes clear the certainty of all of these desirable
blessings that the soul can enjoy. He has given us, step by
step, the kind of assurance that makes for all of this.

It is quite clear, as we have studied this psalm so far, that
David has an assurance that all of this is going to happen to
him. He does not ask tremulously and cautiously and fearfully. He says, "Purge me . . . I shall be clean." He says,
"Wash me, . . . I shall be whiter than snow," and he begs for
forgiveness with the assurance that it will come. He seeks
joy and gladness and rejoicing, and he knows without ques-

tion that God is going to give them to him, so there is in this psalm, from beginning to end, a grand note of assurance. Nowhere does he have a pessimistic view toward God's willingness to bless and to heal and to cleanse and to awaken the old joy in his soul. Surely no one of us, in any part of our land, need be pessimistic or fearful as we approach God.

If we learn nothing else from this grand psalm, we can at least be assured that God listened to David, who had gone so deep in sin. He will listen to your cry and mine. If he could bring all of these blessings to David, surely he can bring to you and to me not only the same blessing, but even richer ones now that his Son, the Lord Jesus, has lived and died and risen again and is at the right hand interceding for us. This is increasingly true in the light of the presence of the Holy Spirit, who makes it his glorious business to find you and me and make us desire just what David desired and make us willing to call out for help, even as he inspired David to plead for these blessings.

Surely, friends, there are treasures unspeakable available for each of us. The Holy Spirit wants us to have them. He guides us to the entrance of the treasure room. He takes us and places us on our knees before a God of mercy and forgiveness. Surely we can find not only the method of salvation, not only the method of restoration, but in the fullest sense the assurance that mercy and grace are plenteous and available and powerful in their creative force.

V. Create a New Heart (Psalm 51: 10)

David continues this heart-searching prayer with a request for a new heart and a new life. Not until Nathan came to him with the parable and the piercing "Thou art the man" did David realize how sin had ruined his life. Since Nathan's visit and since a night spent in remorse and genuine repentance, David has been able to look objectively into his heart and life and to recognize the tragic destruction which sin had brought.

Not only is there poison throughout his whole system, not

only is there a dread infection that permeates every area of his body, mind, and heart, not only is he now a leper badly ruined by sin's touch, not only is his moral nature badly twisted and warped, not only have many glorious months passed while he is still missing the aim, not only does he have a great mark of rebellion and sin against him on God's book, but David realizes fully that his moral nature, his mind, his heart, must undergo a radical recreation.

Hosea will be a bit more vivid in his description of the power of sin when he declares that sin cuts the optic nerve of the soul and renders the soul incapable of making moral distinctions. How tragic it is when sin comes in and settles itself upon the delicate optic nerve which God has created for the soul and in the course of time makes that soul utterly helpless in forming ethical and moral distinctions.

David realized that in the course of that year he had become increasingly dependent upon rationalization and excuses and mental gymnastics that were designed to relieve the pressure of conscience and to give him a semblance of self-respect. He realized that even though misery has been his and the joybells have gone out of his life that something more serious has happened. In some uncanny way the Holy Spirit revealed to David the destructive power of sin.

How precious it is to us if we would but look into the depths of David's treatment of that significant element in our search for victory. Sin has had its way and a terrible wreck has come as a result of it.

David stands and with open eyes looks upon the wreckage and counts up the damage and realizes that he is utterly helpless to make it again as God had created it. Again he is wise and this time he says, "Create in me a clean heart, O God; and renew a right spirit within me." He realizes fully that God can do it and that God will do it.

We find here that David, under the inspiration of the Holy Spirit, is laying the foundation for the New Testament doctrine of the new birth. David was in a sense catching the germ of the idea of the new birth, being born again from above. He realizes that in order to be a new creature he must have the creative act of God evident in his mind and heart. He wants to be free from the shackles of sin. He wants to be freed completely from the bondage of sin and the power of sin. He wants to be freed from the taint and the soiling of sin. He wants to be freed from sin's foul odors, but he also wants to have a brand new heart in order that life from now on might be beautiful and that life might take on something of the divine quality as he moves out to please the God to whom he had been praying.

In a moment of sheer daring David begs God not to banish him from his presence. He has been so unclean that even as a leper God had a right to send him off to a concentration camp where he would be completely removed from clean individuals. He has been a rebellious sinner and has placed himself beyond the provision made for sinful people and God has a right to banish him, even as he banished Cain from his presence.

David realizes now, as never before, that he is utterly unable to live away from the Holy Spirit. He knows without question that life would not only be empty and meaningless, but actually impossible without the guiding and leading of the Holy Spirit. He wants the Holy Spirit to be his guide, to direct his steps, to interpret the meaning of history, the meaning of the Scriptures, and the meaning of definite words of direction. He wants the Holy Spirit to encourage him, to lift him, to sustain him, and he wants life to be a continual round of successes. He knows there are to be no successes in his life unless directed by the Holy Spirit. He knows perfectly well that he is asking for a great boon and yet he is aware of the fact that God will delight to answer and give that blessing.

Again we urge ourselves to be mindful of David's assurance of victory in every one of these petitions. He knows full well that he can depend upon God's promises, and his faith, that has suddenly grown exceedingly strong, dares lay hold on these promises of God.

How much more can we who have Christ as our Saviour expect great fulfilments and enjoy rich blessings as we keep our hand in his and as we walk confidently, guided and upheld by the Holy Spirit. We look in faith to him. He will not only forgive and cleanse, but will make our hearts new again that we may live as new creatures in Christ, walking triumphantly and being more than conquerors through him that loved us.

VI. A UNIQUE VOW (PSALM 51: 13–15)

In the sheer joy that floods his soul David promises to tell of God's goodness. The first impulse of a saved soul is to tell others of the remarkable remedy he has enjoyed. David declares that he will seek out his friends, the sinners who have gone astray, just as he had wandered in sin. He now knows the grace of God. He understands the joy that comes as a result of being saved. He knows that God's grace is plenteous. The rest of his life now is going to be spent in telling sinners that they have fallen, that they need healing and cleansing, and that God is ready to save. He will have such wonderful things to tell of the mercy of God that these friends will be compelled to repent and to confess their sins and to come to him for cleansing.

David will be an evangelist, a seeker after lost souls. He will want them, he will walk with them, he will warn them, he will woo them, he will win them, he will give them assurances of the same kind of joy and blessing which he now enjoys. The gospel he will preach is the New Testament gospel of God's love and grace. The rest of his life, then, is to be spent like this. As an evangelist he will open his mouth and sing and witness to men everywhere of the grace of God.

It is refreshing to find such reaction springing from the new sense of joy and gladness which he now has as his most precious possession. The most unbelievable thing in Christian circles is that men who have been forgiven and cleansed and renewed are so silent and so useless as witnesses of God's grace.

One wonders about the sincerity of a confession and the efficacy of the healing and the depth of the spiritual life when this particular vow is neglected. Seemingly the very first thing any one of us would want to do is to break forth in joyous telling of the story of redeeming love as it has found expression in our own hearts and lives. How anyone can do otherwise is a mystery still unsolved.

If we could call David back this morning to stand by our side and recount the experiences of grace in his own heart, we would be amazed to find that his complete story of salvation involves this reaction which would send each of us out to witness to the saving grace of our Lord and Saviour.

If we learn nothing beyond this from David's experience with God's healing touch, perhaps we will go from this place to do the thing that he promised God he would do. David was certain that these sinner friends of his would not only listen to what he had to say, but be willing to bow humbly and reverently in confession. Again that assurance of his comes to rebuke our lack of faith. Surely we can have more of it as we witness for our Lord.

CHAPTER VI

FORGIVENESS AND SATISFACTION

OUR STUDY OF David's pathetic prayer for pardon has awakened in us a genuine desire to know what the sequel is. As we watched David writhe and sob and pray, and as we heard him make his vow that his whole life would be spent trying to make amends and to tell others of the marvelous remedy which brought joy and gladness to his heart, we have looked expectantly to the solution and have hoped that he might find the kind of deliverance that would fill our own souls with joy.

Surely our world needs the kind of answer inquiring souls would ask concerning forgiveness. As we turn to the answer, it will be our joy to pause for a few moments in considering Psalm 130, and then for a few brief moments Psalm 40, and then continue our investigation as we watch David's beautiful description in Psalm 32 of what happened to his soul. Will you pray that God may give rich assurances to your own heart and prepare you in mind and heart to warn others and then to bring assurance to them concerning this most vital matter?

I. PLENTEOUS REDEMPTION (PSALM 130)

Out of the depths have I cried unto thee, O Lord. . . . If thou, Lord, shouldest mark iniquities, O Lord, who shall stand? But there is forgiveness with thee. . . . For with the Lord there is mercy, and with him is plenteous redemption.—Psalm 130: 1, 3–4, 7.

Here we find one of the delightful bits of poetry that has been selected by Luther as among his four choice psalms. He declares that this psalm is one that most nearly approaches the Pauline standard. It deals with a New Testament subject and reveals truths that are strangely like the New Testament message.

During the Welsh revival one of the great preachers translated verse 4, "There is forgiveness with Thee, enough to frighten us." That might well be the theme psalm of this study, "There is forgiveness with Thee, enough to frighten us." In this little poem the author pictures himself as desperately hounded by sin and by danger and by the imminent approach of certain destruction. He realizes how utterly helpless he is and how hopeless his situation is.

In the midst of that danger and that realization the psalmist is suddenly confronted by the fact that a Redeemer is coming. Joy should fill his soul, but instead he is frightened almost past recognition as he realizes that the One who is coming as Redeemer is the Holy One of Israel and that he is the One who keeps the books and knows the heart of the sinner and cannot look upon sin with any degree of allowance.

The psalmist utters fearfully, "If thou, Lord, shouldest mark iniquities, O Lord, who shall stand?" Coverdale has translated this line, "If thou, Lord, wilt be extreme to mark what is done amiss, who shall stand?"

It is a sobering thought to realize that our lives, so utterly out-of-tune with God and so completely twisted and warped by sin's power, must present a terrible picture as the holy God looks upon them. We have been so adept in the art of rationalization, and we have been so complete in our ability to cover up all the ugly sides of our sin-life that it would help tremendously if we could only face the realization that God sees us in our worst state. He knows without question all of these sins and understands how vile the human heart is. Since he is the Holy One, how can a sinner stand before him and how can one who is thus defiled hope to have forgiveness or cleansing or restoration to his presence?

The psalmist begins by praying with all the fervor of his heart that God would forgive. He knows that it is his only hope. He understands that nothing that man can do will avail. He realizes that no ritual, no offering, no priestly work can do anything at all in relieving him of the sin which has him in its grip.

Suddenly the psalmist becomes aware, however, of that

marvelous thought that God has oceans of forgiveness, plenteous redemption, treasures of full forgiveness beyond description. No one else can, no one else will forgive. His only hope is in the hand of the One who is a forgiving God. David reaches almost to the New Testament level when he has revealed to him the assurance that God is a God of forgiveness and of plenteous mercy. He is aware that love always finds a way, that even as Hosea made it possible for his wayward wife to be brought back with full forgiveness, so would the eternal Lover provide the price and extend the forgiveness that Israel needed.

David knows perfectly well that he himself needs this forgiveness. Calmed and reassured in his hour of agony, he reaches out his trembling hand for the hand of the One who would lift him out of sin and out of despair into the glorious sunlight of forgiveness and cleansing and restoration.

John Newton knew the sublime truth and recorded something of its riches in his immortal hymn:

> Amazing grace! how sweet the sound,
> That saved a wretch like me!
> I once was lost, but now am found,
> Was blind, but now I see.

When the psalmist has given expression to his confession of sin and his cry for forgiveness and the faith that is in his heart as he nestles in the arms of the Good Shepherd, he immediately becomes aware that underneath are the everlasting arms to undergird and to bless. His sins have been forgiven, his hours of misery and conscience prodding have ended, but he will need always about him the great arms of God. He realizes that he has One who can say, "My grace is sufficient for thee," and that throughout his whole life he will be kept and guarded by that eternal Lover who has forgiven and saved him.

In the closing part of this great psalm David pictures himself as the forgiven saint, wholly anchored in a loving God, turning with joy to become an evangelist. He has found mercy and forgiveness and soul-satisfaction, the like of which he has never dreamed could exist. He is thrilled as he feels his feet on solid ground. Why not tell others of his matchless security? He knows the forgiving heart of his eternal Lover. He is immediately set to tell others so that they may know and experience this joy and come with the deepest satisfaction possible to human hearts. The old story of plenteous salvation for all is a story that will be his theme song all through his life. *Plenteous redemption*—what an arresting phrase! There is enough for all, enough for each, enough for me.

> Plenteous grace with Thee is found,
>   Grace to cover all my sin;
> Let the healing streams abound;
>   Make me, keep me pure within.
> Thou of life the fountain art,
>   Freely let me take of Thee;
> Spring Thou up within my heart,
>   Rise to all eternity.

David has become aware of his presence in the arms of the Good Shepherd. He will always hold on to him and will be conscious, as long as he lives, of the debt he owes the Good Shepherd as the everlasting arms are about him and the forgiving love within him.

It will be our joy to continue telling the wondrous story of plenteous grace. As we witness, others will know and come to the fountain of life for cleansing.

II. THE EXPERIENCE OF GRACE (PSALM 40: 1–2)

I waited patiently for the Lord; and he inclined unto me, and heard my cry. He brought me up also out of an horrible pit, out of the miry clay, and set my feet upon a rock, and established my goings. And he hath put a new song in my mouth, even praise unto our God: many shall see it, and fear, and shall trust in the Lord.—Psalm 40: 1–3.

In the fortieth Psalm David gives us an intimate and colorful picture of his experience of grace. We are greatly interested in recent days in experience meetings. A pastor finds it good to call upon some young person who has been stirred by some recent spiritual experience to come before the congregation and give a statement of what God has done for him.

David, seemingly, is doing that for us in throwing on the screen a picture of his own salvation. It is a clear picture of what happened when he found himself utterly helpless, in danger and in imminent peril. He called loudly unto God for mercy and deliverance. We can imagine that he has only recently enjoyed the rich experience such as Psalm 51 would project for us, and the joybells are ringing with new resonance in his heart. He knows what it is to be saved. He is mightily stirred, and he is happy to have the privilege of telling what happened when the Lord took over. Transforming grace is his theme and the love of God glows in the darkness, bringing a miraculous lift to the one who dared keep on calling until God heard and answered.

The psalmist begins by saying, "I waited, yea, I waited expectantly for God." He was not only urgent in his call, but he was patient to listen, knowing that God might come in some way other than the most obvious, and he was determined to be ready in whatever way he might come. He tells us that the Lord brought him up out of the pit of destruction and out of the miry clay.

What a glorious thing it is to have the announcement that when he turned wholly to God that God, first of all, inclined his ear to him, leaned over as a mother would lean in the direction of a child or bent down so that the cry of the sufferer could be heard clearly! When God listened, immediately his great heart responded so that the picture of the Good Shepherd is re-enacted in the case of this sufferer, who recognizes that sin is behind all of his difficulties, and knows that the great love of God is available.

The next line says, "He brought me up also out of the pit of destruction." God's arm was long enough to reach to the deepest depth of the mire. He was strong enough to lift the penitent sinner. He had it in his heart, because love was alive there and in the combination of might and love he found victory.

The note of triumph in these words brings joy to our hearts. The one who was mired in sin, the one who was held by sin's power, the one who was weakened by sin's grip, now was pulled from the grip of sin's master and freed from the peril which had been clearly the way to death and to destruction.

David may be using figurative language, but he is describing a literal deliverance. Nothing in all his life was quite as vivid or as clearly etched on his mind as the bitter night of repentance and confession and prayer for cleansing. Psalm 51 fits in perfectly, not only as the background of this brief word, but as the very picture on which this blessed word is superimposed. David knew what it was to be helpless in the grip of sin. He now rejoices that God is not only able to deliver, but that God's great heart has brought him to this moment of deliverance.

The next word tells of the further step in that blessed experience as he describes the solid rock under his feet, the anchor in the moment of storm, the security, the soundness, the stronghold on which David will be able through all the years ahead to live a life that will please his divine Lord. We can almost hear David as he said, "Yea, though I walk through the valley of the shadow of death, I will fear no evil: for thou art with me; thy rod and thy staff they comfort me." He knows that he has footing that is firm and secure. This precious treasure for a man in an hour of trouble and distress was worth more than anyone could describe.

III. A New Song (Psalm 40: 3)

And then David declares that God has put a new song in his heart. That fresh theme of praise finds expression in a new song. One wonders why so many people go through life without a song. It is tragic to be so completely miserable that the song will not come. How about the music in your soul? How about the song in your heart?

We are not surprised that David had a new song. As a matter of fact, it would surprise us greatly if one who had enjoyed such an experience as David describes could go away without a new song in his heart. We may be sure that the song, which started the day after his confession and after his deep prayer to God, was a song that flowed on unceasingly as long as he lived. He understands fully that behind it there is an unfailing reservoir to feed it and to keep it rolling out in tuneful measures.

God is the one who gave this song. No human could create such a song and make it the triumphant shout of thanksgiving that was evident in this. Praise and thanksgiving poured forth into the air to lift and bless and encourage everyone who came in contact with it.

That song which David sang was not only an expression of gratitude that was as deep and fathomless as his deepest soul, but it was a song that told eloquently of the matchless security that was his now that his feet rested on solid rock and now that he felt the grip of the divine hand on his hand in the dark or in the light.

That song also told in graphic manner of God's method in dealing with penitent sinners. It should be a clear word of direction to all of us. It should provide for a sinner the one way toward forgiveness and salvation and satisfaction. It should make possible a faith fed by the eternal streams from God's presence, so that those of us who have been Christians for a good while may have our faith deepened and our confidence and courage strengthened. Our songs, which have been weakened by distress and difficulty and confusion, may then be clear and powerful in our witness to a world that needs such assurance.

Just as Paul and Silas sang at midnight, and the Philippian jailer, together with all of his prisoners, was led to know and accept the Lord Jesus, so David declares his song will have exceptional effect upon those who hear his singing.

It is tragic that men and women and young people who claim to be Christians have never yet realized that the song born of gratitude because of forgiveness and salvation ought to be a continual witness so that everyone who sees us and hears us can be influenced to look to the source of the same salvation and satisfaction that has been ours.

The most unbelievable thing about us as Christians is that

we can be silent about the greatest miracle that ever came to us. The thing that we will never be able to explain, either to the world about us or to our Lord, is that we can accept salvation and enjoy the fruits of salvation without announcing to the world what the Lord has done for us.

David declares that his life is going to be a continual announcement of the wonders of grace and that as long as he lives he will sing forth praises unto the God of love and forgiveness. May the study of this brief word from the psalm inspire us to breathe forth our song so that others may know what is really deep in our hearts.

IV. The Joy of Forgiveness (Psalm 32)

> Blessed is he whose transgression is forgiven, whose sin is covered. Blessed is the man unto whom the Lord imputeth not iniquity, and in whose spirit there is no guile. When I kept silence, my bones waxed old through my roaring all the day long. . . . I acknowledged my sin unto thee, and mine iniquity have I not hid. I said, I will confess my transgressions unto the Lord; and thou forgavest the iniquity of my sin.—Psalm 32: 1-5.

The classic picture of David's forgiveness and the consequent joy that is his is recorded for us in this thirty-second Psalm. Let us read again reverently and thoughtfully Psalm 51 and make note of each of the fervent prayers uttered by the penitent sinner. When we have listed them, we will come quickly into the rare atmosphere of this psalm and realize that with a shout David announces that all of his prayers have been answered and even more wondrously than he had dared imagine. God has come into his life and restored not only the life, but the joys and the music of his soul.

Augustine loved this psalm above all others. We are told in his journal that quite often he would read it with his heart and eyes pouring forth weeping. During the last months of his life he had it inscribed on the wall opposite his bed so that he might read it and be blessed by its assurances. Out of it grew a quotation that is worthy of a place by the side of each of us. "The beginning of knowledge is to know thyself to be a sinner."

Augustine had been a vile sinner, and this psalm seemingly revealed so much of his own inward struggle and the picture of God's redeeming grace that every time he read it he found his heart swelling within him with rejoicing because of God's goodness and grace. Perhaps that can happen in your life and mine. Surely it was David's hope that it might influence many in his generation and all succeeding generations to turn to God with thanksgiving and prayer and dedication.

In this poem we have the song of a man who is singing aloud his joy because of personal restoration. He praises the Lord, first of all, in a sudden outburst of shouting. He reveals the fact that he has suffered much and sinned grievously, and that he is of all men best qualified to describe what happens to a sinner who repents and confesses, and is forgiven. Quite frankly he pulls aside the curtain and lets us look into his soul as he struggles on through almost a year of bitter wrestling with sin and with conscience.

Not until Nathan came with his direct charge was David awakened to the point that he would do something about it. Up to that moment he had walked among his family and among his people with the definite attempt to convince them that he was clean and noble, and worthy to be their leader. Not until Nathan came did he realize that he was a thorough-going hypocrite. He had rationalized his actions and had outwardly declared that he was all right. He knew in the deeper recesses of his soul that he was all wrong. Now he has ceased to pose before the people around him and has become honest with himself, with his neighbor, and with God.

We do not wonder that David's heart ran over with inexpressible joy as he realized that he was free now from all of the sham and hypocrisy and posing that had characterized this year of suffering under God's heavy hand. In order that we might be thoroughly prepared to know the way to such joy he goes quickly and thoroughly into the task of describing the way to joy. Forgiveness and salvation are possible for anybody anywhere, and his descriptions of the process make it clear to any of us. He wants us to know that, like Bunyan's character in *Pilgrim's Progress,* it is thoroughly possible to have the great burden of sin rolled off one's shoulders that it may find its way into the bottomless pit.

As a free man, David is shouting his word of rejoicing and describing the way of restoration by confession and making clear God's readiness to forgive. Since he has been restored and since the joybells are ringing, he has a strange new access to God. He is doubly assured that in every trial and in every moment of suffering, he will feel the strong arm of God about him. He will not only be strengthened for duties, and upheld in hours of suffering, but he will feel definitely the guiding hand of God as he walks the way and finds the pitfalls that are planted for his feet. He feels definitely that God is a great stronghold and that he, as God's child, can be assured of absolute safety and security in the midst of all of the currents and all of the storms that come.

1. A Father Willing to Forgive

In order that men everywhere may know how much joy is possible the psalmist tries to tell in language that all of us can understand the methods of God in dealing with sin, in dealing with sorrow, and in dealing with guidance. He declares that God is always ready to forgive, always powerful to deliver, and always willing to guide.

Such assurance will change the whole life of a man. No matter how deep in sin, no matter how far he is engrossed in business or pleasure of worldly pursuits, no matter how his head is bowed under suffering or distress, no matter how many the difficulties that arise, he can be assured of the loving presence of One who is able and willing to deal with sin or sorrow or distress.

In other psalms we find reference to the fact that not only is God the one to give the answer in dealing with sin or sorrow, but that in the hour of death he is the one who has the answer and who will provide all of the resources necessary in either of these three emergencies.

To those of us who have the New Testament there should be no question about the solution of problems connected with these three hours in one's life. The Lord Jesus has come to take David's soul-cheering expressions and fill them with new light and new hope as his love and mercy provide the fullest deliverance and the fullest blessings.

David goes about telling the way that one may become the possessor of joys such as he has experienced. He tells us definitely that forgiveness comes only by penitence and that the person who expects to be forgiven must come exactly as he came in that never-to-be-forgotten experience.

(1) *Three words for sin.*—In the first paragraph, verses 1 and 2, David describes his own experience in receiving the grace of God. He refers to sin under three titles: *pesha,* which is literally a breaking away from God; essentially it is rebellion and deliberately doing that which God has forbidden. The word *hatah* is the definite deviation from that which would please God. It is missing the mark or the aim. The word *awon* is literally a misdeed or a distortion or a perversion. It is crookedness or a warped condition that has come about by yielding to the temptation to break God's laws.

David knows that the sin in his heart has manifested itself in all three of these aspects. He has been rebellious, he has broken God's law, he has deliberately separated himself from God because of wilful rebellion. Just as truly he has recognized in his life the tragic result of missing the mark or the aim. Just as one who fires a rifle or releases an arrow from the bow, he has directed his life. The blueprints or the specifications which were prepared for him have been missed completely as he looks back on his life.

David realizes that sin in his heart is that sort of sin, and then he is just as conscious of the fact that the result of these two other aspects of sin is apparent in his life now, when he recognizes perversion or iniquity or a warped condition that is wholly unpleasing to God. It is this sin in all of its completeness that David confessed.

(2) *Three words for forgiveness.*—Even as David used these three titles for his sin, we find him using three words to describe God's forgiveness and to tell what God did with this sin he found in his heart. Forgiveness is called "a lifting up" or "a taking away." The figure has to do with being borne away by a vicarious sacrifice. The second title he uses is the word "covered." He declares that the Holy One who does not dare look upon sin and does not like to have it in his sight covers it so that it becomes invisible to holy eyes.

The third title is the word "canceled." The account book has recorded many transgressions, many sinful deeds, an attitude of mind and soul that hurts God's heart. After prayer and after repentance and after confession David found that God was willing to wipe the slate clean and to erase even the record of the sins that he had committed so that they would not be imputed to him or recorded against him.

So in this picture sin is described as having been taken completely away, having been covered so that it is forever out of sight, and having been canceled as a debt is canceled and no longer reckoned against the sinner. Is there any wonder that the sinner is happy and that he is shouting aloud his thanksgiving to God! His sins are completely forgiven, they are gone from him forever. The debt which had been stored up against him is now canceled. He is at peace with God.

As we look back upon these brief words concerning sin and concerning forgiveness, we are rejoicing in the thought that even though we are guilty of transgression and have departed from God and broken that union with God by rebelling against him and by wandering far away from him, we have a Friend who in all of his holiness is still able to make it possible for us to come back to him again.

Even as the prodigal son broke away from his father's house and selfishly demanded his own way and his father's goods so we, who are prodigals, can always find the way back even though we have rebelled and separated ourselves from the Father's house.

When we face the picture of missing an aim, we are hurt

in heart because we are sure that in every life there has been enough of this to cause our hearts to cry out for mercy. How sorely we have missed the aim! How tragically we have failed in measuring up to his command for us and his purpose for us!

But in David's third picture of sin we find that separation and rebellion and missing the mark find their expression in something that is twisted or distorted. We may rebel against God, we may break the straight standard of law and duty, and as a result of it we may wind up twisted and perverted individuals who need the touch of One who is capable of setting all of it right.

The three steps in the way back are just as beautiful. The psalmist declares that it is our privilege to call upon One who lifts and bears away the load or burden of sin, who covers, as one might cover a foul thing, the sin that it may no longer be present to offend the eye of a holy God. At the same time he blots out even the record in his great book so that in Christ, who makes all of this possible, we may have the kind of forgiveness that will bear our sin completely away and cover it so that not even God's eye will see, and clear the record so that in the Lamb's book of life the fearful blot of early years will be removed so that no trace of them will be found.

How was this done? That is exactly what David is trying to tell us. It is through divine forgiveness, it is because of God's love that he bears away, covers over, and does not reckon to man his rebellions or his errors or his missing the aim. He does not reveal any more the crookedness or the perverseness or the warped nature, because he has forgiven and forgiven completely.

We face one little half line that gives us the secret. David said, "In whose spirit there is no guile." He seems to indicate that the only person who is able to qualify in that great experience is the one who has been so completely pardoned and so completely cleansed that sin has been removed forever.

The great eternal Saviour who came as "the Lamb of God,

which taketh away the sin of the world" (John 1: 29), and about whom it was said, "This is my blood, . . . shed for many for the remission of sins" (Matt. 26: 28), works the miracle. It is in him that we live and it is through him that we are saved.

If your sins have not been taken away by the Lamb of God, they still remain. If you have never laid them on Christ, they are a crushing burden on your heart. Unless your sins have been covered by the atoning blood of Jesus, they lie as an ugly splotch in the presence of God to cry out for punishment.

If you have been independent enough to let your sins mount up and to become many on the book about his throne and have never begged for forgiveness and cleansing and for removal of those sins, they not only stand against you on his record today, but they will stand in the hour of judgment. We know perfectly well that *the blood of Jesus Christ cleanses from all sin.* David knew it even back one thousand years before Jesus came. He has described for us the marvelous gift which God has in store for us.

2. *How David Behaved*

In verses 3-4 the poet takes a leaf out of his book and describes for us his misery during the hours of stubborn, wilful silence. He refused to acknowledge his sin to himself and to God. He continued to bluff and pose and play the hypocrite, seeking daily to convince himself and all his neighbors that all was well.

The psalmist says, "When I kept silence, my bones waxed old through my roarings all the day long." No confession came from his lips, and so night after night he could hear voices in his inner soul accusing him of his vile deeds. No sleep came; remorse and dread burdened him. He says, "Thy hand was heavy upon me."

What a tragic picture it is of a stubborn, silly, misguided man who had this sin in his heart and who was unwilling to let God take it away and cover it and erase the tragic record!

He chose to cover his own sin and to keep silent about it. He refused to confess or acknowledge it. Sullen silence brought increasing misery. For many months God sought to bring him to his knees in sincere repentance. In spite of this he obstinately refused to surrender. How stubborn a man can really be when he has sin in his heart!

David reveals the breath-taking experience that was his when he finally said, "I began to make known to thee my sin and my iniquity did I not cover." He finally came to realize, perhaps after Nathan's charge, that the only way to peace and forgiveness and life was by way of confession. When he ceased to cover his own sin, it was possible for God to cover it for him. When he ceased to carry his own sin, it was the moment for God to take over and carry it. When he ceased to continue to store up new records for his own sinful deeds in God's book, it was possible for God to come with his divine eraser and remove the record of those sins.

One wonders why men would be stubborn and refuse to let God in when all that God seeks is something that will help and bless and lighten and bring joy to the heart.

Immediately David shouts, "Thou forgavest." The "thou" is an emphatic pronoun placed there expressing something of the immediate response of God when his confession was spoken. We could well imagine that less than a split second elapsed before God came with the healing touch and brought forgiveness to his heart. David had finally learned God's way to victory and peace and forgiveness.

Surely his words in this psalm will continue to be a warning against stubborn silence and an encouragement to come to him who forgives and redeems and saves. The author of Hebrews has given us a challenge in those immortal words, "For we have not an high priest which cannot be touched with the feeling of our infirmities; but was in all points tempted like as we are, yet without sin. Let us therefore come boldly unto the throne of grace, that we may obtain mercy, and find grace to help in time of need" (Heb. 4: 15–16).

We are rejoicing at the thought that David's burden fell off immediately. God had heard his humble cry and without a moment's delay had not only granted full pardon, but had performed the entire miracle that transformed him into a new creature. This picture of sin committed, sin concealed, sin confessed, sin covered, sin forgiven, and sin canceled is a picture that will always be needed when we confront men with the necessity of repentance and confession and bring them to their knees before an eternal God who has pardoning grace for everyone who will come in that manner.

3. Victory!

David declares, in his grateful testimony, that he has had not only forgiveness and deliverance, but that he has a peaceful trust in God who guarantees now to make security possible in the hour of storm or in any other experience of life. He declares, also, that guidance will be available in every step that he takes.

As newborn Christians you and I will need the guiding hand and voice of the Holy Spirit. We will not only need the initial act of forgiveness and restoration, but we will need the sheltering arms of the great protecting Father God, and we will need the directing voice of the Holy Spirit, who will make it possible for us to walk triumphantly and confidently in witnessing for him and in carrying out his will as we go.

David also reminds us of a note of rejoicing that is in his heart and that will continue to be in the hearts of all those who have put their trust in God. It is a great experience to be forgiven, to be cleansed, to be restored. Listen to God's Word to one who has been restored, who declared that as Teacher, as Guide, as Leader of his own redeemed ones, God will bring, and his testimony will continue to bring, others to the same source of blessing and to the same One who can provide salvation and life eternal.

If you have had this soul-changing experience, if you have taken your sins to him, if you have confessed them and begged for cleansing and forgiveness, if he has come gladly and quickly to take them all away and restore you to the joy that he alone can give, why not be more concerned about teaching transgressors his way? Why not witness, day in and day out, to everyone with whom you associate? There is no sermon that is as powerful in bringing a sinner to Christ as the sermon that is preached by one who has been redeemed and who tells in direct, colorful language what the Lord has done for him.

In Psalm 32 we have the model. If that has happened to us, then let us continue in all our contacts to express something of the joy and something of the gratitude that well up within our hearts. Surely God has been good to us! Out of sheer gratitude we will continue to tell others, and in telling find increased joy for ourselves and find others coming to him for that same rich blessing that has been ours.

CHAPTER VII

FAITH, COURAGE, AND SERENITY

MEN HAVE ALWAYS tended to fear. Unknown ways, darkness, perils, and adversaries have brought fear to the heart of peoples of all generations. When we go to the Psalms we find a number of exceptionally beautiful words concerning confidence and faith in God. We are face to face with a number of them that declare that God is sufficient and that fear need have no place in godly hearts. Psalms 3 and 4 give us two beautiful gems that ought to inspire confidence and courage for any.

I. MORNING PRAYER (PSALM 3)

But thou, O Lord, art a shield for me; ... I cried ... and he heard me ... I laid me down and slept; I awaked; for the Lord sustained me.—Psalm 3: 3–5.

The third Psalm is a morning psalm, while the fourth is picturing the evening of that same day. The psalmist is in grave peril, adversaries are on every hand. They mock him. The night is coming on and darkness adds its mystery. It also provides its opportunity for evil men to do their worst. In the midst of all of this danger he becomes conscious of the fact that Jehovah is his shield, his glory, and the One who lifts him up. He is aware of the fact that God is not only near, but that there has been established a mysterious communication between the two so that he says, "I cry," and then almost immediately follows the statement, "He answereth."

In the next moment we are face to face with the language of courage. The palmist has slept and awakened, because Jehovah has sustained him. Jehovah has not only been conscious of his frail constitution and the dangers that confront him, but he has been aware of his need for divine love and helpfulness. He has heard his cry. The psalmist is exceedingly grateful now that he has awakened in health and

strength and safety. He knows perfectly well that it was because God's hand was upon his pillow, because this almighty
hand had been reached out under his head.

There is now no need for fear because God pledges his
protection during the night and during the day and through
all the days ahead. The psalmist knows that he can have this
unruffled calmness because Jehovah sustains him unceasingly
and upholds without ever letting go.

II. Evening Prayer (Psalm 4)

> *I will both lay me down in peace, and sleep: for thou,*
> *Lord, only makest me dwell in safety.*—Psalm 4: 8.

In the fourth Psalm, verse 8, we have come to the evening
of that same day. The hard day is over, the strain has taken
much from the feeble man, but now victory has been won,
confidence has increased. He knows that all day long God has
delivered him, that even as he protected him during the pre-
ceding night he has blessed him all day, and now as he lies
down he can rest without fear, realizing that the sleep which
is his is the gift of God who makes him to dwell free of care
though in the wilds of the deep back country of the Jordan.

The psalmist knows that he will need no guard. He will
fear no evil, because he is surrounded by the very arm of
Jehovah and kept in the sweetest peace by the divine hand.
The very fact that he is alone adds to the beauty of it, because
the security that is his now is a God-given security, and the
faith which he now has is the result of his grip on God. He
finds his joy, his satisfaction, his peace in God alone.

The last line sounds almost like the cradle song of a loving
mother who is soothing her tired little one to sleep, knowing
that such a lullaby will make for the best rest imaginable.
"In peace will I both lay me down and sleep" (ASV).
Though alone, he knows that he will dwell safely. These
beautiful words are samples of that which is typical of the
saint who, through rich experience, has come to know that
God is dependable and that he will keep and bless and make
even the night watches safe as his arm enfolds him.

III. Hope (Psalms 16: 9–11; 17: 15)

> *In thy presence is fulness of joy; at thy right hand there are pleasures for evermore.*—Psalm 16: 11.

> *I shall be satisfied, when I awake, with thy likeness.*— Psalm 17: 15.

These beautiful passages reveal to us something of the blessed hope which the psalmist had as he rests comfortably and securely in the consciousness that he is being held now in the arms of God and that he will continue to be forever so kept and guarded and blessed. These verses in the sixteenth Psalm were quoted by Peter on the day of Pentecost and by Paul at Antioch in Pisidia, and in each case the reference is made that they are a prophecy of Christ's resurrection.

Guided by the Holy Spirit, David was able to look forward to Christ. He was conscious of the fact that over him death could have no dominion. He had such fellowship with God in this life that his spiritual eyes were able to pierce the veil for a moment and realize that there is not the possibility only, but the certainty of a continued life of conscious fellowship with God throughout eternity.

In the seventeenth Psalm the poet is not only declaring his faith and his confidence, but making a contrast between his own spiritual hopes and confidence and the low desires of worldly men who are about him. He would not in any sense trade places with them because the things they are enjoying are but for a moment, while his is for eternity.

The psalmist declares he will not be satisfied until he has come to possess not only an eternal peace and joy, but the actual sight of the form of God. He is going to awake out of a sleep one day and there God will be directly before him, and he will be transfigured into the likeness of the One whom he has loved through the years. He cannot imagine that God will be good to him in this life and give him the blessed fellowship that is so precious and then cut him off suddenly and without allowing him continued communion after death has come as a brief interlude.

It is a far cry from the average Old Testament conception of life beyond the grave, but it is thoroughly possible for one who was in touch with God to have the Holy Spirit reveal to him some of the riches which were to be given through Christ after his coming.

The poet declares that he is gloriously alive in the faith that makes him the possessor of something that is eternal and something that will continue past the grave. We are looking right into the heart of Old Testament faith. The future life which these saints occasionally glimpsed was wrapped about the actual presence of Jehovah, God of Hosts. The New Testament faith was the same except that it was clarified and beautified by the teaching and the assurances of Jesus Christ himself.

Whether in the Old or in the New, the faith does the same for an individual, because it assures him that Jehovah God wants his own to rest in him, to hide himself in him. When face to face with death or in the midst of fiery trial or under the load of a heavy burden, he believes that God, who is infinite love, has provided for him not a temporary bit of shelter, but an eternal resting place that combines security and satisfaction and the blessed presence of God himself.

IV. SERENE CONFIDENCE (PSALM 27)

> *The Lord is my light and my salvation; whom shall I fear? the Lord is the strength of my life; of whom shall I be afraid? ... In the time of trouble he shall hide me in his pavilion: in the secret of his tabernacle shall he hide me; he shall set me up upon a rock.*—Psalm 27: 1, 5.

In the twenty-seventh Psalm David gives expression to a peace that has swept over him in the midst of foes and in the certain prospect of persecution and threatened death. He is far from home and has a right to be discouraged. From an earthly point of view there is no hope for him. In the face of all of this, however, he reveals not only a firm faith but declares that his greatest desire is that he may continue in the presence of God, gazing with adoration and rapture upon his face, being strengthened by communion with him, and being encouraged to go out even in the midst of dangers to do the things that will further the kingdom of the One he loves so devotedly.

It is rather remarkable that David has such a faith as this in the midst of so much distress and trouble and opposition. He declares, however, that "He shall conceal me in his pavilion in the day of trouble, he shall hide me in the hiding place of his tent, upon a rock shall he lift me up." With that kind of security and with that sort of hope he has no fear of the future.

David is giving us the antidote for fear. He needs to know that God is near. All of us fall down somewhere along the line and under certain provocations, but the consciousness of the immediate presence of the loving Father God is sufficient to drive all fears out of our mind and heart and life. It is this assurance that buoys up the heart of David and transmits to those of us who need in our generation the kind of strength that will make the going easier for us.

V. The Way to Faith (Psalm 28: 7)

The Lord is my strength and my shield; my heart trusted in him, and I am helped: therefore my heart greatly rejoiceth: and with my song will I praise him.—Psalm 28: 7.

The psalmist utters his word of thanksgiving, first of all, and then turns immediately into prayer. Faith has given him the assurance that Jehovah is nearer and dearer and more available than any help on which he can rely. He has been in suffering. He now finds that this suffering turns into a lilting song, and the song continues until it becomes pure praise. In all of it there is expressed a faith that is transmitted to men and women of our generation. He has given us not only his own testimony but has revealed to us a method by which we can reach the same height and become acquainted with the same Helper and be equipped to sing in the same manner.

VI. TAKING REFUGE IN HIM (PSALM 31: 1–5)

*In thee, O Lord, do I put my trust; . . . For thou art my
rock and my fortress; . . . Into thine hand I commit my
spirit: thou hast redeemed me, O Lord God of truth.—*
Psalm 31: 1, 3, 5.

In this beautiful psalm David is saying to God, "I have
taken refuge in you." What a picture it is of a great man, a
king, a psalm writer, fleeing as a bird into the arms of a loving God! He says about him, "Thou art my rock and my
fortress and for thy name's sake thou will lead me and guide
me."

How beautiful it is to know that David has not only trusted
God completely by throwing himself into the arms of his
God, but that he is counting on daily guidance that will
make his life richer, fuller, and more like the Master's ideal
for it! He then utters the sublime line which has been whis-
pered in the closing moments of the lives of millions of
saints since that day. It was on the lips of our dear Lord the
moment before he gave his life back to the Father. "Into thy
hands I commit my spirit."

These words are too sacred for interpretation. The psalmist takes his own body and mind and spirit in his trembling
hand and hands them over to God. This precious treasure
that he is committing to the Father is a deposit which God
has engraved and which is in the truest sense precious, because it is God's creation. It is precious, also, because it is the
only body and mind and soul that the psalmist possesses, and
he wants all of it to be kept and blessed by the hand of God.

Since Jesus sanctioned and consecrated these beautiful
words they have become increasingly precious to the saints
through the ages. May they be for us today a challenge that
will lift us clear out of our shallow, selfish, self-centered lives
and cause us to commit our best for him.

Kings and peasants alike find refuge and peace in the Lord
God of truth. May men today commit their spirits to the
eternal God who is our Rock and our Fortress.

VII. Joyous Assurance (Psalm 34: 4, 7–8)

*I sought the Lord, and he heard me, and delivered me
from all my fears . . . . The angel of the Lord encampeth
round about them that fear him, and delivereth them . . . .
Blessed is the man that trusteth in him.*—Psalm 34: 4, 7–8.

In the heart of this lovely psalm we have a testimony from
the psalmist who is happy in the thought that God has done
so much for him, and he is concerned about telling of it so
all may know and rejoice. His faith is calm and buoyant under circumstances that shake the very foundations of life.
He proclaims joyfully, "The angel of the Lord encampeth
round about them that fear him, and delivereth them."

What a note of triumph that gives! He has just declared
that Jehovah hears and answers and delivers and makes
radiant and saves and keeps and redeems. Now he says that,
"The angel of the Lord encamps round about them that
fear him and delivereth them."

How good it is to know that we have that mysterious Being, who in some strange way in Old Testament times was
considered to be Jehovah's representative in dealing with
men. We have him about us, watching, protecting, blessing
by his very presence. He is like an army encamping all
around the city to defend it or like a host of angelic beings
at the command of God, thrown like a great protecting guard
all around to assure absolute safety and security. Perhaps
there are ministering angels alert to every need of one who
is in distress or in need or who has a special prayer on his
lips.

The psalmist has declared already in his testimony that
some friends of his have experienced something of this same
blessing and when they turned their eyes of faith upon God,
they met an immediate response and their faces were bright-
ened or made radiant as they looked upon him. They received something from him that made them capable of standing all the tests of the days ahead without being confounded
or put to the blush with disappointment. He declares that

when he called, God answered and saved him out of every distress of his heart.

The psalmist immediately turns to us and says, "O taste and see that the Lord is good; blessed is the man that trusteth in him" (34: 8). "Blessed is the man that taketh refuge in him" (34: 8 ASV). What a beautiful line it is! How marvelous it is to have a faith like that, to have a grip on God such as the psalmist has!

Can it be yours? Is it possible for one in our generation to have a faith so clear, so gripping? It seems it should be much easier for us to have this faith, since we have the Lord Jesus Christ as our Redeemer and as our Saviour. He has said, "I am with you alway, even unto the end of the age" (Matt. 28: 20). Paul has said, "We are more than conquerors through him that loved us" (Rom. 8: 37). How much more easily can we in our day hold fast to the faith that is so colorfully presented in this brief selection from one of David's psalms?

David's reference to the Angel of God's presence calls to mind the Old Testament story that tells us of Jacob, encamped in a lonely place, and after a rich experience with God through the night, he called the place Mahanaim, "two camps" (Gen. 32: 2). He tried to get across to us the meaning that alongside his little camp there was another. He said, "The angel of the Lord encampeth round about them that fear him and delivereth them." David's little camp was poorly garrisoned and the enemy might easily break through his human guard, but outside that ring is another guard through which any intruder must break before he can get at him.

It is a thrilling thought! Jesus went even further and said, "Neither shall any man pluck them out of my hand." A sentence or two later he says, "No man is able to pluck them out of my Father's hand" (John 10: 28–29). It seems that when we are in Christ, we are doubly safe, because we are first in Christ's hand and then Christ's hand is in God's hand and so, hidden as we are, we are thoroughly safe from anyone's reach. It is almost the picture that David gave utterance to in this beautiful line which has become so precious to all of us.

VIII. A Proved Recipe (Psalm 37: 3–5)

Trust in the Lord, and do good; . . . Delight thyself also in the Lord; and he shall give thee the desires of thine heart. Commit thy way unto the Lord; trust also in him; and he shall bring it to pass. . . . Rest in the Lord, and wait patiently for him.—Psalm 37: 3–5, 7.

The psalmist in this poem is an old man and instead of facing life with a cynical view, that seems to have been the lot of Solomon when he said, "All is vanity," David gloriously says, "Trust . . . delight . . . commit . . . rest . . . wait." He declares that the best antidote that he has ever found for fretting and discontent is patient trust in Jehovah and a quiet following in the steps which God has marked for him.

These three verses give us a prescription that reveals so many good riches that it is almost a tragedy to try to deal with them in a few lines. The psalmist has decided that fretting is not only wrong, but that it hurts one and that it is unavailing, unnecessary, and unbecoming. He says, "Trust in the Lord, and . . . delight thyself also in the Lord; . . . roll thy way upon the Lord. . . . rest in the Lord, and wait patiently for him."

You can see immediately that David is dealing with a fundamental recipe that will work in anybody's life. If we trust fully in the Lord, life will be different. Our attitudes, our affections, our wills, our behavior, will be different.

The psalmist declares then that the way toward peace and tranquillity is that we shall delight ourselves in the Lord, knowing full well that he will give us the desires of our hearts. That one word guarantees full freedom from the slavery imposed by earthly, sensuous, selfish desires. If we would live lives of full happiness, we will seek to be thoroughly pleased with God's desires for our lives, knowing that in that way we will find the kind of life that will be deepest and fullest and richest for us.

When that is done, David declares that we must "roll over on him" our way. The word "commit" is good, but the words "roll over on him" is a literal translation of the verb, and when we have done that we have guaranteed that we will be free from the perplexity of choosing our own path.

Would you like to be free from the burden of making all of the decisions as to the choice at the forks of the road? Would you like to have the best guidance that anyone can imagine for life's journey? The psalmist declares that his God is dependable and that in that particular capacity he will give the final word of wisdom.

The fourth word that David has for us in his prescription is the full remedy for impatience. If you would have a calm faith, he declares that you must "rest in the Lord." That means to be silent before the Lord in the calmness of faith. This particular part of the prescription guarantees that the future is not uncertain for you any more since you are leaning on him. Whatever else there is in life, whether turns in the road or confusing crosspaths, the guide directs the way and brings full assurance to us that he will be there in that unknown future.

In another psalm the writer declares that a home is prepared for us at the end of the journey. The prescription is to *trust* in the Lord and *delight* one's self in the Lord and *roll over on him* the burden of guidance, and *rest* comfortably and trustingly in him, *waiting patiently* without fretting and fuming for the full working out of his plan in our lives, knowing that at the end of the trail he will not only be present, but a home prepared for us by his own loving hand will bring joy to our hearts.

This psalm is a literal jewel for saved and unsaved alike. If one among us has not found peace in Christ, there is no hope for the things which David describes until he has met the conditions. For those of us who have committed our way to the Lord and rolled over on him the leadership of our

lives, there can be nothing short of faith and trust and hope
and confidence. Each day will unroll before us with the same
bit of surprise and adventure and unknown quality, and yet
it will bring increasingly the consciousness that we are trusting One who knows the way, who knows our frame, who
loves us devotedly, who has a purpose for us, and who is
working out that purpose through us.

IX. "HE IS THINKING ABOUT ME" (PSALM 40: 17)

I am poor and needy: yet the Lord thinketh upon me.
—Psalm 40: 17.

One sometimes finds a gem in the midst of a thicket. This
seventeenth verse of the fortieth Psalm is a precious treasure.
It was brought to our attention once by a great English
preacher who stood quietly for quite a while looking at the
audience, his white hair glowing, his face alive and challenging. Then almost without effort his lovely voice spoke
these words, "I am poor and needy: yet the Lord thinketh
upon me." The effect was electric! No one of us who heard
it will ever get away from the impression it made. For us that
verse has become a priceless treasure.

Perhaps the psalmist was not aware of the great effect the
verse would have in human hearts down here in the twentieth century. He has given expression, first of all, to a marvelous experience in his own life when he was saved, and
has made it so vivid and so colorful that we have rejoiced in
it, but from there on sorrow and distress and fear have
mingled one with the other until we have decided to lay the
psalm aside and seek for better help in other poems. Suddenly this one line hits us between the eyes. "I am poor and
needy: yet the Lord thinketh upon me."

Will that help you? Does it help to know that even though
you are unknown, unimportant, a little cog in life's rolling
machine, yet in God's eyes you are an individual? Not only
does he single you out for thought as an individual, but as
one precious enough for him to give his only Son to die for

you. He is thinking about you even though there are more than two billion people on the face of the earth. You may not be too high in the list of those two billion, but our text declares that God is thinking about you. What is he thinking? What are you thinking? Personally, this verse has done and always will do something to my heart.

X. Our Refuge (Psalm 46)

> *God is our refuge and strength, a very present help in trouble. The Lord of hosts is with us; the God of Jacob is our refuge.*—Psalm 46: 1, 7.

We reach the climax of the shout of confidence and victory when we come to this great psalm. It has exerted such tremendous influence in the life of Christian leaders through the centuries that we can take time to look into its powerful message for our hearts. It took hold of Luther in such a way that it practically made his life a burning, fiery, irresistible fagot.

Oliver Cromwell said about it, "It is a rare psalm for a Christian. 'God is our refuge and strength, a very present help in trouble.' If Pope and Spaniard and devil set themselves against us, yet in the name of the Lord we shall destroy them. 'The Lord of hosts is with us; the God of Jacob is our refuge.' "

As John Wesley lay dying in London many thoughts clamored for utterance, but his closing words were, "The Lord of hosts is with us; the God of Jacob is our refuge." All through the centuries, these heart stiffening words have put courage and stamina and confidence in the hearts of those who would dare stand up for Christ and for Christianity in the face of opposition, in the face of seeming destruction.

The psalmist was moved by some signal display of God's power and might. Perhaps it was the deliverance of Jerusalem from the hated Sennacherib and his army in 701 B.C. when a hundred and eighty-five thousand soldiers lay dead on the battlefield as a result of God's hand upon them. At any rate the author of this psalm has become tremendously stirred and he dared to announce to the people that the God who was able to bring about such a great victory will be available not only for the armies of Israel, but for every single individual among them all through his life.

It is a shout of triumph! It is a prescription for confidence. The psalmist has dared take hold of Isaiah's announcement concerning Immanuel, which is literally translated, "God with us," and dares claim that in this recent signal deliverance God was in the midst of the city.

We who stand in the bright light which has been cast from the person and the sacrifice of the Lord Jesus, can in the fullest sense claim that God is with us, because we have the presence today of the Holy Spirit. The confidence which was generated in the mind and imagination of the psalmist can be multiplied many times over for us who can feel the very presence of the Holy Spirit as he directs our activities and encourages us to go forward toward conquests that are more marvelous than any of the Old Testament battles.

XI. SUBLIME TRUST (PSALM 56: 3)

What time I am afraid, I will trust in thee.—Psalm 56: 3.

A little gem that must not be left out is found in this out-of-the-way place, literally singing its song to our hearts. The psalmist said, "On the day when I might have ground to fear, I will cling trustfully to my God."

We sometimes feel, perhaps, that fear is not a sufficient reason for faith and we are apt to disparage the kind of faith that comes when one is afraid. Someone has said that each day of peril should be to him a discipline of faith.

What about your life and mine? Does your faith grow when fear comes? Is it true that fear is a good stimulus for faith? Why not let fear cause us to have faith? When he had said this, the psalmist goes on to say, "In God have I put my trust, I will not be afraid" (ASV).

David was in a very bad spot with all of the enemies of Saul surrounding him, hunting him, and ready to put him to death. It is a tragic hour in his life and David declares that he is going to be honest and give us the occasion of his trust. He said: "It was a day when I was most afraid, when I was frightened almost to death. I did not have any cause for confidence or faith, but there was a deep sense of need. I did know that I was exposed to danger. I did understand that of myself there was no way to victory, but I said I *will* cling trustfully to thee."

All around David nature was crying out, "Be afraid." His enemies sought in every way possible to drive home the lesson that he ought to be afraid, but David said, "I will trust and not be afraid." It was the occasion of his faith and surely there is nothing for David to be ashamed of there. As a matter of fact, David is the person who introduces us to it in the Old Testament. "I will trust" is a brand new idea until David presents it as his contribution to the theology of the Old Testament. The word "trust," as David uses it, means to "cling to," or to "hold fast to anything." After all, that is faith, whether in the Old Testament or in the New Testament or in the twentieth century. It is faith when one clings, holding onto God through Christ.

Not only does this little verse introduce us to the occasion of faith and declare for us what faith really is, but it assures us that faith has the victory. He says, "In God I have put my trust; I will not fear." All of the enemies are still in the woods looking for him. Everybody would help cause fear, but he has his faith in God and is clinging to God and on that basis fear is impossible.

The psalmist is in position now to assert himself and declare that his will is at work, because his eye has been taken off the danger and placed on God. His soul literally clings to God and so there is no occasion for fear. He knows God will be enough. He believes that the trust that he has imposed in him will bring about the victory that will continue to keep fear out of his life. It is the same as we hear in later years, "This is the victory that overcometh the world, even our faith" (1 John 5: 4).

XII. A Fixed Heart Sings (Psalm 57: 7)

My heart is fixed, O God, my heart is fixed: I will sing and give praise.—Psalm 57: 7.

Think with the poet of a miserable night of fear and hiding and constant alarm, of enemy troops passing and fearful threatening. When fear has made the body as weak as water, there springs forth just at dawn a new faith and a new courage and the psalmist shouts, "My heart is fixed, my heart is fixed, I will sing and make melody. I will give praise, I will awake the dawn, I will give thanks to thee, O Lord."

In the fifty-seventh Psalm we see the strange contrast in the life of a fugitive who found courage and strength and whose heart became fixed as he caught sight of the presence of God and felt the grip of his hand upon his own. The night had been dark, dangers had been about him, but now he is ready to start singing and he calls on musical instruments to join him.

Usually the poets of the Old Testament spoke of the dawn as waking individuals. This time David declares that he will steal a march on the dawn and do the waking, because his heart, being fixed, must sing. He would remind us that a fixed heart sings. One who has faith in God, one who puts his trust in God and clings to him, claims the kind of strength that not only makes him stand triumphantly, but makes him want to forget his own peril and shout his praise and thanksgiving to God who has given him the deliverance.

XIII. I Am Continually with Thee (Psalm 73: 23–28)

Nevertheless I am continually with thee: thou hast holden me by my right hand. Thou shalt guide me with thy counsel, and afterward receive me to glory.—Psalm 73: 23–24.

The seventy-third Psalm is one of the greatest of the entire collection. In order to take this particular section and see the sheer beauty of its message we would need to study the entire psalm, because it is a vital part of the woven fabric of that beautiful poem.

We must let it suffice, however, to mention the fact that the psalmist had suffered a great deal of difficulty in seeing the prosperity of the wicked while realizing his own piety and his poverty that went along with it. Seemingly misfortune had dogged his steps while the wicked had been blatant in their infidelity and had received showers of good things day in and day out.

His faith had well nigh gone on the rocks. It was a tragic hour for him. How could a faith stand such a shock. He was on the point of renouncing his faith and turning completely away from God because he felt that God had no more use for him and would do nothing else for him.

One day the psalmist decided to go into the sanctuary and there he found a full solution to his problem. The verses of our chosen text come as a result of his visit to the sanctuary and the vision which God gave him. First of all he saw the transitoriness of the prosperity of the wicked and the tragic end that would come to wicked man. Also, he was startled to find that he himself had treasures far more precious that he had imagined.

God was able to make the psalmist realize that he was still a choice possession of the divine heart and that night and day he had been immediately by his side and that no hour had passed without the divine presence to make possible guidance and security. God had been near for protection, for sustaining, for nourishment, for guidance at the crossroads, for driving out fear, for exhaustion, and had proved himself the God that any human heart would want.

Now the psalmist realizes that in the midst of all of life's roar and rush he had been continually with God. He even finds that God has been holding his right hand. He is aware now that God has sought to guide his every step. He is even able to reach out beyond this life and for a moment catch a supernal picture of the other shore and he dares say, "Afterward receive me to glory." A moment later he says, "It is good for me to draw near to God: I have put my trust in the Lord God."

It is worth all the millions for a man to have an experience like that. No one of us realizes fully that our lives are protected and guided and guarded and kept by the unseen but eternal presence of God himself. When we have finished seeing that, we may be just as poor, just as far from earthly prosperity and popularity, but when we realize that we have his gracious nearness, his supporting grasp, his unfailing counsel, his directing finger, his royal welcome into the heavenly home, something happens in our hearts.

This psalmist went back shouting aloud in triumphant notes his love for, his faith in, and his devotion to a God who had been with him all the time and who would hold him close through all of life's fitful way, and then into another world he would be taken to remain as close and as securely blessed as ever in any of his life.

Perhaps your life and mine need the tonic of this tremendous truth. In the midst of confusion, in the midst of shallow thinking, in the midst of prejudices and selfish desire, it becomes easy for us to imagine that God is not very good to us and that he seems to be as good to some blatant sinner as he is to us. We are tempted to ask the question, "What does it matter and what do I get out of it, and how am I in any better position than my neighbor who lives an open life of sin?"

This psalm will solve the problem. These words will send us back to the sanctuary, back to the holy place, back to our knees, back to God. It is there that any one of us will find that the nearness of our eternal Father God is the most precious possession that we can claim. We are brought near to him through Jesus Christ, our Saviour. When we have accepted him and placed our trembling hand in his nail-pierced hand, then we are near, and we will always be near in this life and throughout eternity.

Even when we are called to go through trials and danger, he will be near to sustain our spirits and guide us into paths of righteousness and usefulness.

XIV. PSALM 91: 1–2, 11–12, 14–16

> *He that dwelleth in the secret place of the most High shall*
> *abide under the shadow of the Almighty. . . . He is my*
> *refuge and my fortress: my God; in him will I trust. . . .*
> *For he shall give his angels charge over thee, to keep thee*
> *in all thy ways. They shall bear thee up in their hands, lest*
> *thou dash thy foot against a stone.—Psalm 91: 1–2, 11–12.*

When one tries to deal with the ninety-first Psalm, he is conscious of the fact that the less he says the better it will be. It is simple and direct. It describes the security of the godly man and the protection of a loving Father amid the perils of a dangerous journey through life. There are some statements, there are some promises, there are some assurances. Perhaps we can take a few lines to call to our mind the richer portions.

In verses 1 and 2 the theme is presented. Anyone who takes shelter under the wings of Jehovah will be secure always. He is an almighty Guardian. One who comes in that fashion will be treated as God's guest. The almighty wings will be spread around him during the night, and no danger will have power to touch him.

The psalmist is trying to make clear that all of the power of God is at the disposal of a fugitive who flies, frightened and pursued, into God's sheltering arms. Nothing will be kept back, every bit of the power which God possesses will be thrown about him for his protection and safety. Let us remember that it is simple trust in God, clinging to God for protection, that makes all of this power and this protection possible. The psalmist says, "He shall shelter thee with his pinions and under his wings shalt thou take refuge. His truth is a shield, a buckler."

The section that has to do with the guardian angel is especially attractive to our minds since it was quoted by the tempter when he was dealing with Jesus in the mount of temptation. Listen to the psalmist as he says: "For he shall give his angels charge over thee, to keep thee in all thy ways. They shall bear thee up in their hands, lest thou dash thy foot against a stone." Whether the devil had any right to claim him or not, we shall let others discuss, but as needy creatures we have always claimed the right to hold it as our own possession.

From early childhood days it has been a treasure for our hearts. It cheers us to think that our lives are in God's keeping and that he thinks enough of one of us to send all of the hosts of angels to keep us from stumbling and falling! As we look about us and realize the number who stumble and fall and go astray, we are made to pray even more earnestly that all of these shall be made conscious of the fact that God wants to shelter them under his wings, because it is not his will that any of them should stumble. He would love to see the cleanest and finest and most victorious of all creatures walking in his love and meeting his requirement and triumphing as creatures who trust and cling to him.

The closing part of the psalm is rich because "he hath set his love upon me, therefore will I deliver him." That is the Word of the Lord. He is talking about this individual who has set his love on him. Then he says further, "I will set him on high, because he has known my name."

There are two things about the man that God likes especially. One of them, "he has been in love with me," and second, "he has known my name." That is, he has known the inner meaning of that holy name and has had the kind of reverence for it and the kind of understanding of its sacred, mystic meaning that has brought out from his mind and heart those qualities that are evidenced by love and by devotion and by dedication. He closes with this beautiful word: "He shall call upon me, and I will answer him: I will be with him in trouble; I will deliver him, and honor him. With long life will I satisfy him, and shew him my salvation."

All of these boons are to be desired. Each of them is a treasure all its own, but when we put them all together along with those in the New Testament revelation, we gain a new and larger appreciation of God's promises in these words to the one who is willing to trust.

If you trust and if you love and if you are fully acquainted with God's name, he is ready to fulfil his promises not only to protect you and shield you and keep you, but with all of these richer things, he is willing to honor you, setting you on high and making you free from trouble. He will honor you beyond any way of describing the height of it and then show you the fuller and richer meaning of salvation. Surely it must be yours! These words are meant for you and for me.

XV. "UNTO CHILDREN'S CHILDREN" (PSALM 103: 17–18)

But the mercy of the Lord is from everlasting to everlasting upon them that fear him, and his righteousness unto children's children; to such as keep his covenant, and to those that remember his commandments to do them.—Psalm 103: 17–18.

Even though we have studied Psalm 103 in the psalms of praise and thanksgiving, we must think for a moment of the assurance and comfort that come to us from several of these verses in this psalm. The eighth verse for instance, "Jehovah is merciful and gracious, slow to anger, and abundant in lovingkindness" (ASV). And then 17 and 18, "The mercy of the Lord is from everlasting to everlasting upon them that fear him, and his righteousness unto children's children; to such as keep his covenant, and to those that remember his commandments to do them."

One of the thoughts that strikes us with peculiar force is that even our grandchildren are guaranteed a special blessing by the loving Father who is so precious to us. Fathers and grandfathers try to provide financial help and education for sons and daughters and grandchildren, and here the psalmist declares that no matter what we do in our own earthly way, God guarantees definitely that even to the children's children his righteousness will be poured out.

How precious it is to know that God, the One who is like a Father, the One who knows our frame, the One who remembers that we are dust, the One who in gentle lovingkindness cares for us, is looking after us, and will care not only for us, but for all those who are dear and precious to us.

Chapter VIII

LONGING FOR GOD AND HIS SANCTUARY

WE HAVE ALREADY learned that the psalmist loved the Scriptures and was greatly exercised in his desire to have all others know and love them. Next to his love for the Scriptures his enthusiasm for God's sanctuary looms largest. We are sure that he was not concerned altogether with the sanctuary as such, but that he was so thrilled with the thought that in God's sanctuary he would be close to God and, being there, he would be able to worship God in the beauty of holiness.

The psalms we shall study reveal an intense longing for God's house. All of this is in the light of the fact that the Temple had so little to commend itself as an attractive meetinghouse. The Temple was a harsh and stern place, where bulls and oxen and sheep and goats were slaughtered and where blood ran freely while the smell of the slaughterhouse went throughout the entire building. In addition to this disagreeable feature, the pilgrims had a long journey to make and no conveniences of any kind.

We wonder today how the brethren from all over the Convention journeying to the annual meeting would do if they had the kind of disagreeable journey which confronted those who went up to the house of God. They faced a dry and hard and thirsty land with almost no water on the journey. They traveled on foot and slept out on the hard ground at night. Many days were consumed in this fashion, and no luxurious hotels awaited them at the end of the journey.

In spite of all of this there was great enthusiasm in the hearts of men when they thought of going up to God's house. They did not look forward to sermons or to great inspirational addresses, but something happened to their hearts when they thought about Jerusalem and when their minds turned to the feast days. They lived a hard life, suffered much, were lonely, and a great deal of sadness crept into their hearts as the years went by. The one bright spot seemed to be when they could leave home and journey all through the rough country to God's holy place.

I. HIS SANCTUARY (PSALM 84)

> *My soul longeth, yea, even fainteth for the courts of the Lord: my heart and my flesh crieth out for the living God. . . . Blessed are they that dwell in thy house: they will be still praising thee. . . . Who passing through the valley of Baca make it a well; . . . They go from strength to strength. . . . For a day in thy courts is better than a thousand. I had rather be a doorkeeper in the house of my God, than to dwell in the tents of wickedness. . . . Blessed is the man that trusteth in thee.* Psalm 84: 2, 4, 6–7, 10, 12

Psalm 84 gives us something of the longing in the heart of one psalmist who describes his hopes as he thought of this trip and the experiences that were his on the journey and the blessings that would be available for those who could not go, but who had it in their hearts to go. The last part of the psalm deals with the pilgrim's prayer and the consciousness of the privilege of meeting with and talking with God, who is a source of unfailing blessing for everyone who trusts him.

We look at this psalm as a poem coming from the heart of one who loved Jerusalem, who loved God's house, and who loved God. In all of this love there was a great longing to be where he could feel God's presence and find a rich blessing for his heart.

It was on such a trip that Jesus, as a twelve-year-old boy, found the great gathering for worship in the Temple so stimulating that he could not pull himself away from it to go home with his mother. The opportunities and privileges that were his as a young lad made him forget everything else for three full days and remain in that atmosphere, rejoicing in the fact that he was close to the sanctuary and close to his Father God.

If we do not learn other lessons, perhaps we will be able

to learn what a tragic loss members of our churches suffer when they forsake the assembling of themselves together. They could, if they would, look back and realize how in history the group of humble people at one of these Jewish feasts found the kind of enrichment and enduement that made for religious fervor and spiritual growth.

One day at Pentecost, as the peoples had assembled from all over the land, the Holy Spirit came in mighty power to fill and to overflow all those who were in touch with him. Perhaps in your church, in your meetinghouse, the Holy Spirit is waiting for your coming to pour out his blessings upon you and upon those members of your families and others who come along with you. What a responsibility it is! What a privilege we have!

The author describes faith as having a mighty anchorage in God, and that same faith becomes active and lives in a mighty way in the hearts and in the groups of people as they travel. It finds a rich assurance day by day so that instead of finding men weakened by the toils of the road, they go from strength to strength, becoming more confident daily that they are soon to appear before God and find the enduement that comes from his own presence.

The psalmist declares that those who dwell in God's house are exceedingly happy and are blessed beyond any way of describing it, and at the same time he goes a step further and says that even those who cannot go, if there is a great desire in their hearts, will be richly blessed. If in their heart are the highways, then there is a blessing for them also.

II. "Passing Through"

The psalmist's third word is, "The man who trusteth in thee is blessed." His threefold benediction then is upon the man who is able to go, the man who wants to go, but who cannot, and then the man who has a great abiding trust in God. Whether he goes or stays, he is the one who finds the riches that are unspeakably precious. As he describes the journey, we run into this beautiful expression, "Passing through the valley of Baca he maketh it a place of springs; yea the early rain clotheth it with blessing." No one will ever know perhaps exactly what is meant by that phrase "the valley of Baca." The word *Baca* means weeping.

What about the figure, "He maketh it a place of springs"? The thought that becomes most apparent to us, as we study, is that this great group on their way to Jerusalem, passing through the valley of desolation and sorrow, have within themselves what it takes to bring a blessing to those who are encountered along the way.

So much of our life is taken up with "passing through." You go to the office, you go home, you go to school, you go to a distant city, you are on a Pullman, or you are driving. What is your attitude while passing through? How much do you help? What do others gain from your presence?

Jesus was not only anxious about those of his disciples, but he was constantly giving himself that his "passing through" periods might mean much to someone else. You remember, he was talking one day by the side of the well to the woman who had come for a pitcher of water. That ministry is a ministry that shines more brilliantly than the star of the highest magnitude. It was easy for him to give of the very best teaching and preaching of his life to this poor woman from the village across the way.

Jesus taught concerning this beautiful thing in describing the man who fell among thieves and who was left to die by the side of the road. The priest came along and walked by on the other side. The Levite came along, saw him, and turned and walked on the other side and left him to die. These two men were "passing through." They were representative of so many of us who pass through without taking the responsibility, without accepting the privilege, without lifting and helping, without saving a life.

Jesus tells us that a Samaritan came along and instantly stopped his beast and went to him and administered first aid, wrapped his own cloak about him, and put him on his beast and carried him lovingly and tenderly to the inn and assumed all responsibility for his care. Jesus, after teaching that powerful lesson, asked the question "Which of the men proved a neighbor?"

One wonders just how much we do in hours that are strangely like that hour. The psalmist said that these people passing through the vale of weeping turned it into a place that was joyous and glad, made hearts that were weeping rejoice with exceeding great joy. Our hearts can be turned to that kind of behavior if we love the Lord Jesus enough and if we are thoughtful and concerned about our fellows.

The real reason for going up to Jerusalem was to get close to God. As they talked they were cheered by the joyful anticipation of seeing the holy city, standing within the walls of the Temple, hearing the shouts of hosannas, listening to the teachers as they taught in groups, making their offerings whether large or small, and then coming into vital touch with God. God revealed himself in the sanctuary, even though the worship was not so attractive, and even though the priests in some cases were worldly and professional. A blessing always came to the people who made their way to the sanctuary. They met God and they were never the same again.

It is such a rare blessing to meet God. In his house one can meet him. Perhaps in the quiet moment of meditation, perhaps while the organ music is coming softly and penetratingly into your ear and heart, perhaps during the joyful singing of some gospel song or some stately hymn, perhaps while the Scripture passage is being read, or the sermon is being preached, perhaps as the Holy Spirit speaks during the invitation to church membership, but in all of it God can be found and his message is heard.

How glorious it is to know that this psalmist loved God's house, loved God, and in describing these friends who went up, he was able to say that they went from strength to strength, growing stronger, more zestful, more joyous with every day and that they finally arrived, all of them, at God's house where they would meet him and be moved by him.

People who do not know the secret of protracted meetings or of conventions or of assemblies or of Bible conferences, perhaps discount the sacred influence of such meetings in the lives of those who attend regularly. When people are persistent in their waiting on God, as in protracted meetings or in summer conferences, they are together with their thoughts on one matter and with a continual presentation of spiritual truths that make an impact upon mind and heart.

They face the realities of the gospel or they are looking across the world at tasks or conflicting ideologies that confront the Christian world. In the course of it all they have their minds penetrated, their hearts stirred, they gain new convictions, they are girded with new purposes, they go away from these conferences or away from this series of meetings with a new soul, with a new enthusiasm, with a new commitment, with a new dedication of themselves.

We are sure that if this is true in the lives of those who attend, then men and women everywhere who are absenting themselves from church attendance are causing the opposite reaction to have sway in their hearts and lives. If an exhilarating program of attendance with attention given to spiritual things helps in such a marvelous way, then the absence of any spiritual impressions from church attendance will help cause an atrophy of those things that are worth while and will cause the spiritual springs to dry up so that life loses its zest and one becomes selfish to the point that he is not worth much as a Christian or as a church member.

The truth is a sound one. If our churches could only devise some way of reaching the large percentage of their members who do not attend worship, the churches would have scored a tremendous victory. Smoldering embers of devotion would be fanned to flaming zeal. Spiritual spastics would leap and run in the Master's service. Churches now crippled for lack of workers would find, in the lives of revitalized Christians, the forces needed to launch out in an aggressive warfare against evil.

III. The House of the Lord (Psalm 122)

I was glad when they said unto me, Let us go into the
house of the Lord. Our feet shall stand within thy gates,
O Jerusalem. Psalm 122 : 1–2

The author of this particular psalm lived a long way
from Jerusalem. One day some neighbors told him of a
trip they were planning to Jerusalem and he was invited
to make up one of the party. What a joy swept through
his heart! He was hardly able to contain himself as he
thought about it and as he dreamed about it, as he realized
the wonders and the glories, the blessings of that glorious
city. He had given expression to that beautiful verse that
is so much in the minds and hearts of our people, "I was
glad when they said unto me, Let us go into the house of
the Lord." Surely that has been echoed over and over, and
so many of our good shut-ins would like to be able to put that
into operation today.

The point, however, of richest joy seemed to be when
this man stood in sight of the sacred city and looked at
the Temple and all the buildings of that ancient city. No
one who has not had this experience can begin to imagine
the thrill of it.

Before going to Jerusalem I read quite an extended statement from Dr. Talmage describing his emotional outburst
when his carriage was stopped on the hills on the Mount
of Olives and he was allowed the privilege of looking
down into the old city. I read it two or three times and then
laid it aside with something of a feeling that Dr. Talmage
had either been rather emotionally geared or else he had
indulged in an exaggeration.

I did not think of the statement any more until one
Sunday afternoon, in early April, as we were driving from
Nazareth to Jerusalem. Our driver slowed the car almost
to a standstill as we came to the crest of the hill overlooking
the sacred city. Quietly he stopped the car and sat there
without a word while my emotions, seldom stirred as deeply

as then, became almost unmanageable as I gazed upon the sacred city, the city of God. It is an unforgettable experience in my life.

As the psalmist stood there looking at the majestic city, he was swept by the consciousness that so many world-shaking things had happened, so much that would be forever precious to the minds of men. Then he began realizing what the days ahead might bring, and so without realizing it he broke forth into exultant praise.

What a glorious thing it is to have a city like Jerusalem! The walls are not pretty, the buildings are far from modern, the streets could not be dignified by the use of that word, and yet the holy city, even more sacred now than in the days of the psalmist and destined to be even more sacred in the years ahead, will always call for the best in love and adoration and worship.

The poet was not only aware of the fact that he was in a holy place, but he could sense without question the realization that he was in the vicinity of a sacred presence of God himself. To be sure God was up in the hill country where he lived, but not as he was in the sanctuary, and soon his feet would stand on the very threshold of that holy place. Soon he would be near enough for God to speak to his heart. He bursts forth in praise and prayer and bids all people everywhere to join him in praying and in rejoicing that God in all of his glory speaks to men and will continually speak to men through that experience.

As we think of God may we fall in love with him, may we have something of that same strange passion that stirred in the heart of the psalmist who had Jerusalem in his heart. How he loved the sacred city! How precious were its memories of past greatness, its glories still to be revealed, its holy sanctuary where God was worshiped! Jehovah who gave significance to everything was there.

In his prayer the psalmist extends the wish, as he talks with God, that we might have that same passionate love for God that will cause us to make all efforts to find our place in his sanctuary, to bow our knees in prayer, to open our hearts in worship, to open our mouths in praise as the Master lives in us and as we tell others the world around of his saving gospel.

IV. THIRSTING FOR GOD (PSALM 42–43)

As the hart panteth after the water brooks, so panteth my soul after thee, O God. My soul thirsteth for God, for the living God: when shall I come and appear before God? Psalm 42 : 1–2

O send out thy light and thy truth: let them lead me; let them bring me unto thy holy hill, and to thy taber- nacles. Then will I go unto the altar of God, unto God my exceeding joy: yea, upon the harp will I praise thee, O God my God. Psalm 43: 3–4

When we come to see a courageous soul hounded and worried and dying of thirst, the very best within us rises up. We are brought up from our lazy thinking suddenly by the consciousness that there is a man actually dying of thirst.

The psalmist declares that he is like the hind who has sought earnestly every one of the water holes in that whole area and not even a moist bit of sand is available for her, and in sheer desperation she is left to think of the good, refreshing water that she used to enjoy and to wonder, as her eyes become glassy and her mouth dry like a piece of leather, if there will ever be another sip of refreshing water to cool her parched tongue. The psalmist uses that illustra- tion as he says: "As the hart panteth after the water brooks, so panteth my soul after thee, O God. My soul thirsteth for God, for the living God."

It is a tragic hour when a man who used to know God and who used to enjoy God is wholly separated from him. It is bad enough when illness or infirmity has separated him from worship and from God's holy house. But when one has slipped and backslidden to the point where he absents himself from the worship of God without real reason, it is cause for alarm. When he suddenly realizes how thirsty he is, how hungry he is, how utterly near death he is, simply because of thirst and hunger, it is time for thought, for prayer, for coming back to God.

This psalmist has enjoyed better days. He remembers very well the time when he used to be in God's house. He remembers when he used to have a real place in the great religious festivals. His mind is flooded with sweet memories, while a literal rush of tears washes his face. Now he is helpless, perhaps leprosy or some other disease or some accident has rendered him a thorough-going example of one who is forsaken of God. His neighbors taunt him, laugh at him, jeer, because of his bad lot and ask him derisively, "Where is thy God?"

In the midst of all of this, in the midst of everything that is going on, the psalmist knows that he has just one need and that is the need for God. Augustine said, "Thou hast made us for thyself, and our souls are restless until they find rest in thee." The psalmist knew perfectly well that he would never find rest until he found it in God. He knew that no remedy, no panacea, no man-made gift, could assuage the grief of his heart now that he had been awakened to the consciousness of his thirst for God. Nothing would solve his problem except touch with God.

There is pathos in the groanings of this dear man who, after recalling God's mercy and declaring his utter dejection and his despair, turns abruptly and suddenly to a very passionate prayer for deliverance from his enemies and a more earnest prayer for restoration to the privilege of the sanctuary and God's house. He wants God to take a hand in his situation and help him immediately. He wants him to send messengers, *light* and *truth,* to come quickly to his humble home and take him quickly into the very presence of God.

It is pathetic to think that he was so lacking in the kind of knowledge of God's presence that a New Testament saint would have, but the poor fellow was doing the very best that he knew how, and his prayer is not only fervent and compassionate, but it is grounded in the very nature and grace of God. He has hope, he has an unwavering faith, and he believes, without question, that the God who was so good to him in former years and who has so much mercy for the penitent soul will have mercy in this case and restore and lift and make him see his face again so that rejoicing may be his and the joy of his heart may resound unto the telling of others of what God's grace has meant to him.

V. BEGGING FOR MERCY (PSALM 27 : 7–14; 28 : 6–7)

Hear, O Lord, when I cry with my voice: have mercy also upon me, and answer me. When thou saidst, Seek ye my face; my heart said unto thee, Thy face, Lord, will I seek. Hide not thy face far from me; put not thy servant away in anger: thou hast been my help; leave me not, neither forsake me, O God of my salvation. Psalm 27 : 7–9

Blessed be the Lord, because he hath heard the voice of my supplications. The Lord is my strength and my shield; my heart trusted in him, and I am helped: therefore my heart greatly rejoiceth: and with my song will I praise him. Psalm 28 : 6–7

In the early part of this psalm we were overjoyed to find faith and confidence and courage and rejoicing and fellowship. It seems that when a psalmist is so completely at peace with God and so fully overshadowed with his love and mercy and goodness that he would never come to the state which is revealed in the prayer which he utters in the latter part of this psalm. But the psalmist comes in this last section to beg with all his heart for deliverance. Things are worse and have grown worse so quickly that he is utterly unable to cope with them.

The full thought of God, which we saw in the first half, makes possible the full abandon of the prayers that we find in this section. Since God is light and salvation and strength and since God is the One who hides him and lifts his soul to the rock for an eternal anchor, he is the very One on whom a distressed soul can call.

The one who has been forsaken by his father and mother, who has been cruelly treated by enemies, who has been slandered by those who hate him finds not a single friend anywhere in the whole list of his human associates to whom he can call and on whom he can lean. Surely we will allow the psalmist to break down. He is pleading for his life now. It is a pathetic story. He even imagines that God is on the point of hiding his face from him, but he rises to the heights at the close and, in his own way, reveals his faith in the joyous announcement that Jehovah will take him up. He knows that he can lean on him and that he can depend on him.

In Psalm 28 : 6–7 we are face to face with one who has cried out to the Lord in his distress and who has found an answer. He has trusted fully in the Lord and he has been helped. His heart is rejoicing and his song is going forth in reverent but full praise to the Lord of Hosts. He answers and blesses.

Such a section as this delights our heart as we realize that a psalmist who was so sorely hurt has found it in his heart to repent and pray and confess his sins and find God willing not only to hear, but to come with a healing touch and restore him fully and completely. As a result of this he is shouting aloud his praise and continuing to sing his song of thanksgiving to his great Deliverer.

VI. Agonizing Prayer (Psalm 55)

And I said, Oh that I had wings like a dove! for then would I fly away, and be at rest. . . . As for me, I will call upon God; and the Lord shall save me. Psalm 55 : 6, 16

In this poem we are presented the heart-rending picture of a psalmist who suffered because of the treachery and betrayal of a friend. David had such an experience with Ahithophel at the time of Absalom's rebellion. We do not know that he is referring definitely to this, but it seems to be the identical picture. The poor man is in despair, he is in sorrow, he has full indignation at white heat. He soon finds faith and peace and quiet and victory.

One great commentator has said that there are three

movements. The first one is fear and that soon leads to a desire for flight. The psalmist said, "Oh that I had wings like a dove! for then would I fly away, and be at rest."

The second movement is fury. The troubled heart that has been so sorely crushed breaks forth in indignation and fury, but fury could lead only to hate and some kind of retaliation.

The third movement is the movement of faith, and that alone creates courage and confidence and restores the right relationship with God.

As we study this poem and watch the changing moods of the psalmist and understand something of the victory to which he finally came, we are reminded that God would have it so in all our lives. The hurts and indignities and slurs and slights of life, instead of wounding and making us hard and rendering us less beautiful and more miserable, ought to be taken fully and completely to the Lord. And without any reservation whatever, we ought to dispose of them in prayer and in restitution if that can be possible.

Our Lord suffered something of this same experience in the betrayal of Judas, and some of the later commentators were disposed to think of this as a prophecy of Judas' infamy and treachery. Perhaps we should hold it as David's very own and see how in the heart of an Old Testament saint the victory was achieved without resentment and hatred and hostility. David was infinitely better in his later years as he turned his heart and his talents and his life completely over to God and let God have all that he possessed.

VII. SETTLED IN THE SANCTUARY (PSALM 73)

> *But as for me, my feet were almost gone; my steps had well nigh slipped. . . . Until I went into the sanctuary of God; then understood I their end. . . . Nevertheless I am continually with thee: thou hast holden me by my right hand. Thou shalt guide me with thy counsel, and afterward receive me in glory.* Psalm 73 : 2, 17, 23–24

Perhaps you will go with me as we study the greatest of the psalms and understand something of the way a sincere soul struggled through the dark night of doubt and questioning and emerged finally as a saint who had a firm grip on things that gave him a firm faith.

The poet was guilty of getting hot and bothered because of the prosperity of neighbors who left God completely out of their lives and yet seemed to prosper more than anyone else in the community. He could not understand why these people could be exempted from the common lot of pain and have special privileges in a suffering world and continue their blatant infidelity as they stalked their selfish way across the earth. It seemed to the poet that they had no chastisement or punishment brought upon them.

That particular problem is still a problem in the hearts and minds of our people. The psalmist said that he came very near losing his faith; his feet were almost gone; his slender faith had practically collapsed. He was asking: "What is the good of it and why should I be good? Why should I continue to live a godly life while sorrows and pains and sickness plague me, and all of my life is seemingly wrapped up in misery and disappointment and defeat?"

We do not know how long the man continued in this state. We cannot know how many miserable nights he spent, or how far he went in leaving God out of his life. Perhaps he refused to go to the sanctuary at all. Perhaps he made light of the religion of his fathers and became an outspoken opponent of Jehovah religion. Perhaps he influenced his family to drop out and become pagan in their attitude.

We are reasonably sure that in this state the poet made life miserable for everyone in the home and made the days and the nights unbearable for anyone who was forced to associate with him. Each day the infection grew worse, the misery increased, the doubt grew larger. His decision was almost complete. He would definitely break with the holy teachings of his fathers and become an outspoken pagan.

Then the psalmist describes for us the process by which he found the steadying grip that made him over again. It was not easy. So far as we know, his friends and the other members of the Temple family did not do their part. Maybe he had to struggle on alone, but one day he decided to go to the sanctuary. He had known happy hours there. As he thought back, the only true satisfactions of his life had come from the hours spent in God's house in sincere and whole-hearted worship. He would go again!

When the doubter arrived at the sanctuary, he found that God was already there and that God had a special word for him. It was a word that had to do with his neighbors. The man up the street, who had been so much in his mind during the years, was presented before his eyes. God said, "I would like to show you a little something about this man." He showed him a picture of the man's heart and revealed to him something of the fears and the uneasiness and the disquietudes that ran about during the day and during the night in the mind of the one who seemed to prosper. God showed him that underneath this sham and pose and hypocrisy a troubled soul struggled along.

The second picture God showed was a picture of the latter end. That must have been a terrifying picture. The poet saw his own neighbor plunging off into endless misery and death. What a picture! It had a very terrifying effect on our friend. God let him look at it awhile.

The thought was sobering. After all, why begrudge this man the few puny bits of pleasure that he enjoyed? His life would be snuffed out in just a little while and the terrors of the other world would be beyond description.

At that time God came back to the psalmist with another picture and said, "I would like you to see a picture of yourself." This time he found out something that he had been strangely ignorant of all along. He saw himself in this picture walking the way with the eternal God holding his right hand. How precious it must have been to see and know that life, with all of its burdens, its temptations, and its fears, is made beautiful by the presence of an eternal God who would hold his right hand and walk the way with him.

The psalmist is overwhelmed. How can he hope to live his life of antagonism, his life of paganism? How can he continue to leave God out of his life? Without having settled it fully, God comes to show him one other picture which seems almost beyond the psalmist's day and yet the

language has definitely the statement, and the whole message of the psalm seems to give strength to this interpretation. This picture reveals God as taking the pilgrim gently
by this same hand and receiving him finally into glory land
to be with him. Do you wonder that the psalmist was able
to say in language that must have had a veritable shout in
it, "Truly God is good to Israel!"

There was in his heart now a faith that was so securely
grounded that no slight or selfish understanding of God's
preference for someone else or any feeling of being forsaken
or abandoned could have any influence upon him. From
now on, even though his weakness and frailty and suffering
continued, even though his neighbor continued to live his
wild, godless life, even though his earthbound philosophy
might still sound good in some ear, our poet would be a
triumphant worshiper of the Lord God of Hosts.

Without holding anything back, with reckless abandon,
with joyous thanksgiving, with genuine faith, with triumphant trust, he grasped the hand of his God. Doubt was gone
and joy had come, and faith was now so securely founded
that it would be eternal in its reach.

So much depends on the worship of God in his sanctuary.
This psalmist might have gone on for many months without
ever finding the solution to his problem had he failed to
enter the sanctuary. This poor man might have been miserable and a doubter, a scoffer, a man without a God, unless
some touch of the Spirit had prompted him to enter God's
house.

Surely much depends on worship in the sanctuary. Someone has entitled this psalm "Settled in the Sanctuary." How
many problems, how many sorrows, how many needs have
been settled in the sanctuary? This psalmist found the
answer. This man of God found his faith. This man lost
his doubts and lost his miseries and found in the sanctuary
the rich, abiding faith that came from his touch with God.
May God grant that the study of this psalm may instil in
us something of the sacredness and the sanctity and the
importance of the sanctuary in the life of our people.

Chapter IX

FOREGLEAMS OF THE SAVIOUR

From the earliest beginnings of the Old Testament we find evidences that the Holy Spirit intended to prepare the hearts of the people for the coming of the Messiah. All the way through those centuries that hope was kept alive. The prophets contributed much to the stream and added additional lines to the portrait of Christ.

The long years of the interbiblical period (400 B.C. to Jesus' day) changed the picture and produced new lines in the anticipation of the function and mission and person of the coming One. With all this, the people of Palestine failed to recognize their long-promised Messiah. How dim and vague and imperfect was the picture! Jesus spent much of his time and energy correcting false and imperfect hopes and bringing to the fore the true word concerning himself.

In the book of Psalms we find many references to the Messiah. Other paragraphs picture the results of his reign. Some passages refer to him as God's Son, the chosen King, the anointed Priest. Others contain the germ of the idea made more perfect by Isaiah 53 and helped prepare the way for the Suffering Servant.

In some of the psalms the direct reference seems to be to David or David's son, but many prophecies in these poems could find their richer fulfilment in the Messiah. Others represent Jehovah, himself, coming to the earth to bring judgment and redemption. Whether the Messiah comes as Son or as Jehovah, as King or Priest or Suffering Redeemer, he is to be heaven's answer to earnest prayers and fervent hopes through the years.

In some way all of the following psalms may be considered messianic: 2, 16, 18, 20, 21, 22, 35, 40, 41, 45, 55, 61, 69, 72, 89, 109, 110, and 132. We will not have time nor space to single out the verses and deal with the aspect of truth revealed in each. We shall try to study together the three psalms that are pointing directly to our Lord and find their fulfilment in him.

I. THE CHOSEN KING (PSALM 2)

> *Yet have I set my king upon my holy hill of Zion. I will declare the decree: the Lord hath said unto me, Thou art my Son; this day have I begotten thee. Ask of me, and I shall give thee the heathen for thine inheritance, and the uttermost parts of the earth for thy possession. . . . Be wise now therefore, O ye kings: be instructed, ye judges of the earth. Serve the Lord with fear, and rejoice with trembling. Kiss the Son, lest he be angry, and ye perish from the way, when his wrath is kindled but a little. Blessed are all they that put their trust in him.*—Psalm 2: 6–8, 10–12.

This familiar poem is a psalm of Jehovah's King. There is strong reason to believe that it refers to David and that in a reasonable sense David fulfils some phases of the poem. It is, however, as a typical and prophetic psalm that we deal with it in this study. It is prophetic of the world kingdoms in their rebellion against the kingdom of Christ and the entrance into the fray of the Son of God who is Jehovah's representative against these earthly kingdoms, and finally the triumph of the kingdom of Christ. Jehovah gladly gives him the nations as his own inheritance. He allows him the privilege of winning them. If they accept him and trust him, they will rejoice with him forever. If they rebel and refuse, he must judge them and the judgment will be severe.

In the New Testament we have several references to this psalm. Acts 4: 25–28 quotes it and Paul, at Antioch (Acts 13: 33) , quotes verse 7 as finding its highest fulfilment in the resurrection of Christ. The titles "My Son" and the "Lord's Christ" are familiar New Testament titles.

The book of Revelation has drawn heavily on this chapter to find some of the phrases and sentences that are used in picturing the final triumph of Christ and his kingdom.

In the book of Hebrews, Psalms 2 and 110 are placed side

by side, each being considered messianic. Psalm 110 refers to the eternal priesthood of Jesus, and Psalm 2 gives a testimony of Jesus' sonship above the angels.

The two names for the Messiah, which were in use in Jesus' day, the "Christ" and the "Son of God," find their origin in this psalm. The New Testament teaching concerning the office of the Messiah has a twofold designation. Christ is the One who is the author of salvation and makes it possible. He is also the Judge who brings the final condemnation upon those who refuse to accept him. In his act of redemption he is beginning, and in his role of Judge he is completing his work.

Christ is spoken of as having the scepter of peace and the shepherd's staff and bearing the rod of iron, so it is not untenable to think of this psalm as typically messianic. Much of it was not fulfilled and could never find fulfilment in any person until Jesus came. His coming and his ministry and his death filled it to the full all the way through.

In this psalm we have the picture of the King, who is God's Son, who is chosen to declare war on the devil and his kingdom and to wrest from the devil his power over men. David is truly a prophet of God who predicts the career and victory of the Messiah, the Son of God. We recognize him frankly and unhesitantly as God's Priest-King. We see, in this psalm, David's highest work as a prophet.

The King is seated at the right hand of the Father with all his kingly dignity. He has been chosen by his Father to take over the rule of the peoples of the earth. He has only recently received from the divine hand the prerogatives of the kingly office. He loves lost men and yearns to see the power of the devil broken. He intends to go forth as a warrior to break the devil's power and to set the captives free. In his heart there is a burning passion to save. He will gladly go forth and give himself not only in warfare against the devil, but as a sacrifice to bring back the redeemed ones who have been bound by Satan's chains.

In the last part of the second stanza the Father comes forth to make the announcement that he has just set his own Son over the peoples of the earth. Note the word that is used describing the peculiar equipment that sets the King forth with all of his authority and with all of the prerogatives that go with his office.

Beginning the second stanza, verses 6–8, the anointed One himself begins to speak and announce what he is and what he plans to do and what he will in the end accomplish. It is a joyous moment when Jehovah presents his Son, the King, and when the King accepts the appointment and announces his platform of world conquest.

It will be a battle to the finish. No one will be able to stand before him. He is God's Son. He is the King. Jehovah has destined the sovereignty of the world for his Son. He has shown his willingness to accept and he goes forth with his royal scepter, becoming, if need be, a rod of iron which can easily break any head like a potter's vessel.

The closing stanza is the word of the poet who very frankly advises and exhorts the multitudes of the peoples of the earth to cease their rebellion and to turn in humility and in commitment to the Holy One, Jehovah's Son, the King, the Leader of a new army. He wants them to show intelligence or insight and to allow themselves to be advised, to kiss the Son, to make peace with him, to accept him, to come and fall at his feet and submit themselves to Jehovah, as well as his Son. It is a beautiful poem! May God bless it to our hearts.

II. The Priest-King (Psalm 110)

The Lord said unto my Lord, Sit thou at my right hand, until I make thine enemies thy footstool. . . . Thy people shall be willing in the day of thy power, in the beauties of holiness from the womb of the morning: thou hast the dew of thy youth. The Lord hath sworn, and will not repent, Thou art a priest for ever after the order of Melchizedek.—Psalm 110: 1, 3–4.

Psalm 110 is purely messianic. It was always considered to be so, even in the age before Jesus quoted it in his discussion with those who confronted him in Jerusalem. These rulers of the Jews definitely agreed with him that it was both Davidic and messianic. Jesus points out that David, who in the fullest sense was a king, was in this psalm singing of another who was Lord and therefore superior to himself.

David speaks here as a prophet. There is nothing typical about the psalm. As a prophet of God, he has received a divine revelation concerning the Messiah, which he puts down for all generations and transmits it so that even Jesus of Nazareth might read it and find encouragement in it. He is delighted to say, in this prophetic message, that Jehovah has chosen the Messiah to share his throne with him. He has a great purpose to subdue all the nations of the earth. He has selected the Messiah to do the work of leading the successful invasion. Zion is the seat of that earthly kingdom.

From Zion this newly crowned Priest-King will go forth conquering and to conquer. Young warriors by the thousands will flock eagerly to him and with the strength of youth and the sweetness of devotion and the cleanness of apparel will dedicate themselves to do or die that the King's orders may be carried out and that the worlds may be won to the Lord.

This Messiah who is so clearly pictured is both a King and a Priest. He does not happen to be in the line that was made famous by Aaron, but he has received a special divine appointment after the order of Melchizedek. The King is thus appointed by Jehovah to be King, to be Priest, to be the world Missionary, to lead the multitude of dedicated young men and women to bring about the witness that will conquer the nations of the earth. He finds that his strength is to come altogether from Jehovah. He is, in the fullest sense, to go forth to conquer.

We are happy to bear our testimony that every word of this prophecy is literally fulfilled in Christ. It is a prediction of the exaltation of Christ to the right hand of the eternal Father and also a prediction that he will be victorious over all enemies and over all peoples. Dr. Delitzsch in his commentary agrees that David speaks of him directly and objectively in a prophetical representation of the coming One.

In this psalm we see, first of all, the special announcement from the Lord setting his Son at his right hand and issuing a decree that his rule shall be over all the peoples of the earth. It is a divine decree. It is beyond question the eternal pronouncement of God himself.

The seat at the King's right hand was not only the place of honor, but it was a place that was made for One who was to share the throne with him, to sit close by him, to share his dignity, to have a share of all his authority and power, to be a part of the great ruling power that would take in all peoples of the earth. He, himself, would delight to stretch forth the scepter out of Zion as the new capital and let it reach on out among the peoples of the earth.

The announcement is made rather enthusiastically, "Thy people offer themselves willingly in the day of thy power." It is thrilling to see the multitudes rushing forward to become freewill offerings and to present the best they have in the dew of their youth, in the priestly behavior, in the commitment of all that they possessed. They gladly dedicate their freshness, their inspiring effect upon the King, their immense numbers, the glistening of their armor in the sunshine, the lilt of their song as they go forward, the pouring out of their blood in the holy cause, and the final rejoicing in which they will share as the triumph of the King becomes a certainty when all peoples bow before him.

It is a song with so much imagery, with so much beauty, with so much lift, with so much joyful participation in a victorious crusade, that we find ourselves wishing that we might be allowed the privilege of watching the triumphant Son of God as he goes forth. In majesty he sits by the side of the divine Father and then accepts from the Father the appointment to go on this mission of witnessing and wooing and winning.

We can see literally multitudes swarm to him in adoration, in reckless abandon, in gladsome submission, in joyous commitment, taking their places at his side, eager to follow his lead, ready to listen for his slightest command. One day when the great battle is over and when the devil has been completely eliminated and when the nations of the earth have come to accept our Lord and his Christ, many of us who have a part in presenting our best alongside of him will have joys so unspeakable that we will be almost beside ourselves and our hearts will shout aloud an endless hymn of praise to the Lord God omnipotent who reigns forever and ever.

III. The Suffering Servant (Psalm 22)

> *My God, My God, why hast thou forsaken me? . . . All they that see me laugh me to scorn: they shoot out the lip, they shake the head, saying, He trusted on the Lord that he would deliver him: let him deliver him, seeing he delighted in him. . . . Many bulls have compassed me: strong bulls of Bashan have beset me round. Thy gaped upon me with their mouths, as a ravening and roaring lion. I am poured out like water, and all my bones are out of joint: my heart is like wax. . . . My strength is dried up like a potsherd; and my tongue cleaveth to my jaws; and thou hast brought me into the dust of death. For dogs have compassed me: . . . I may tell all my bones: they look and stare upon me. They part my garments among them, and cast lots upon my vesture.—Psalm 22: 1, 7–8, 12–18.*

When we come to face the reality of the message of Psalm 22, we are confronted with different views concerning the message. One group of scholars would claim that it referred altogether to David and had no meaning beyond his life and experiences. Another group of scholars would claim that it is descriptive of the sufferings of the nation Israel and is fulfilled rather fully in all of the sufferings which the nation endured.

The third group would declare that even though it describes some event in the life of David and is thoroughly grounded in that historical position, yet it is fulfilled only in Jesus Christ of Nazareth, God's Son. It has, in the course of years, become so perfectly associated with Jesus that we can hardly find it in our minds to think of it in any other terms.

This psalm pictures Jesus as the Saviour. The twenty-third Psalm pictures him as Shepherd, while the twenty-fourth gives us a picture of him as Sovereign. We are somewhat influenced perhaps by the fact that Jesus, in his most excruciating moment on the cross, took this psalm and claimed it as his very own, quoting the first verse of the psalm in his native tongue. As the little boy of Nazareth his tongue quoted, "My God, my God, why hast thou forsaken me?"

There are altogether too many literal fulfilments of specific words and images and pictures to make this accidental. David never experienced in detail many of these sufferings. No other person in the Old Testament had anything like such persecution and suffering to bear. The nation certainly fails to fulfil it in anything like an adequate manner.

The only person who ever fulfilled it is the Lord Jesus, and the fulfilment is so exact and so literal and so complete that it transcends even the account of eyewitnesses who stood within twenty feet of the cross and described as eyewitnesses the exact suffering and the words which the great Sufferer spoke. Isaiah in his chapter 53 gives us more in detail and more in descriptive comment of this experience, but even the great Isaiah did not approach this psalmist in the color and vividness and accuracy of detail of the scene about the cross as it is displayed before us.

After having faced every single argument for all of the theories advanced, it is without question correct to study this psalm as the prefiguring of the loneliness, the persecution, the suffering, the death of the Lord Jesus as he fulfilled the prediction which Isaiah delivered in saying, "He was wounded for our transgressions, he was bruised for our iniquities: the chastisement of our peace was upon him; and with his stripes we are healed. All we like sheep have gone astray; we have turned every one to his own way; and the Lord hath laid on him the iniquity of us all."

The psalm begins with a heart-rending shriek of anguish, advances to an urgent plea for help, and comes finally on the uplands into a joyous vow of thanksgiving and rejoicing. Let us begin with verse 1, the pleading cry of the forsaken servant of God. It is out of the question for us to understand all that the psalmist had in mind in presenting this cry at the beginning of his psalm. Faith and despair are wrestling in the psalmist's mind.

Faith says, "My God" and continues to pray. Despair declares that prayer is out of the question, because the poor man is already forsaken. The psalmist does not seem to be calling for an explanation. He is shouting his own word of utter astonishment at the God who has been so gracious and devoted and fatherlike who has turned his back on him and forsaken him in the hour when he needs him most.

As you will remember, the time that Jesus quoted this was high noon when, after three hours of intense suffering on the cross, the Father's face was turned away from him and the windows of heaven were closed and the world was plunged into pitch darkness, the like of which no one had ever seen. It is in this moment that sin comes upon the sinless form of God's only Son, and this shriek of distress and anguish of soul rends the air.

Jesus uses, as has been said, the familiar language of his childhood days. He is utterly astonished to realize that in the midst of the severest agony of all his experience the Father has seemingly forsaken him. In our New Testament study we would be able to explain the reason for this, but in the agony of that moment the Suffering Servant gave expression to the line that was closest to his heart, "My God, my God why hast you forsaken me?" A moment later he said, "Why art thou so far from helping me, and from the words of my roaring?"

When we come to verse 7 we see the rulers and other enemies of Jesus laughing him to scorn. They gape with their lips, they shake the head. Those gestures of contempt and abhorrence and scoffing and hatred reveal much more than we realize, and they hurt the great heart of our Lord far more than we can count.

As if to give direction to the priests, the psalmist says, "He trusted on the Lord that he would deliver him: let him deliver him, seeing he delighted in him." The fulfilment is too literal and too vivid to need comment. It is a wonder of wonders that the chief priests who knew the twenty-second Psalm so well fell into the line quoting it so literally.

When we come to verse 12 we are facing insolent enemies who are called "bulls" and who gather in circles round about the One they are about to attack. These people who surround the cross are spoken of as "strong bulls of Bashan." The psalmist goes on to say, "They gaped upon me with their mouths." What insolent enemies they are! Like a lion roaring as it prepares to spring upon its prey, these men range themselves round about the suffering One and make ready for their ravenous attack upon him.

In verse 14 the psalmist describes the effect of all the anxiety and the persecution. All his body is racked and ruined and tortured. His strength has gone. Much of his human courage has oozed away. He is reduced to a skeleton. He says, "All my bones are out of joint." We are not sure just what is involved in that one line. Perhaps they had used some unearthly machine of evil that helped make him utterly miserable so that he might die sooner and so that his body might be even more to be despised as people looked upon it. He said, "My strength is dried up like a potsherd; and my tongue cleaveth to my jaws; and thou hast brought me into the dust of death." He is nearing death and all of the vital juices of the body are about gone. His tormentors are the instruments of Jehovah and they have come according to the orders of the divine One to execute his will upon him.

The psalmist goes a bit further and says, "For dogs have compassed me." These dogs, unclean, half savage, cowardly, cur dogs, hungry and wild and ravenous, like a band of marauding thugs, have gathered in the immediate vicinity of the cross. Perhaps some of them were not so evil and so hungry and so ravenous and so doglike until stirred up by the priest, but now they have turned all of them into a wild, cruel, dangerous group who will stop at nothing to bring ruin upon him, to cause him to suffer, to execute what they consider the will of God.

The next verse declares that the hands and the feet are

pierced. Seemingly the thought is that these "dogs" have gone so far as to pierce hands and feet. There is no mention of spikes or nails, but the picture is the same.

And then turning from that the psalmist said, "I can count my bones." He is just a skeleton now. There is no difficulty seeing every one of his bones and then to add insult to injury, "They part my garments among them, and cast lots upon my vesture." They are waiting for his death and now that they think he has almost reached that point in the bitter agony, they strip his body, divide his clothes eagerly among themselves, and when they come to this one seamless garment that is not to be divided, they cast lots to see which one will possess it.

We can hardly think of this as happening to David or to any other Old Testament figure. We do know that it was literally fulfilled in the crucifixion of our Lord. We know that this inner garment was made the prize for the one who would win as lots were cast.

Can you imagine anything so pathetic, anything so tragic, anything so cruel and godless, anything so heart-rending, as this vivid, colorful eyewitness account of something that is to happen down through the years? As a boy in Nazareth Jesus was to read it and recognize himself in this eye-witness account of an occurrence which would culminate his earthly existence, which would in effect make perfect the prophecy of John the Baptist, "Behold the Lamb of God, which taketh away the sin of the world," and the words of Isaiah in that matchless fifty-third chapter. How could Jesus read it through those thirty-three years of his life and memorize it so that the vivid details stood out in glowing descriptions and yet go on stolidly and courageously with a set face to that hour when all of this should come upon him?

We now hear the psalmist praying to the God who is still listening. He knows that he is listening. While he is praying and while he is uttering the deepest prayer of his heart to a God who is at the same time his loving Father, suddenly he breaks forth in thanksgiving, in praise, to the One who has delivered him. If we study the fulfilment of all of this, we are most impressed with this particular part of the prediction and its fulfilment. How wondrously the psalmist was able to come to a climax which came so triumphantly on the cross as Christ said, *Tetelestai,* which means, "it is finished," and then a moment later, shouted with a triumphant shout, "Into thy hands I commend my spirit."

The victory is assured. It is not defeat. All of the suffering, all of the mockery, all of the cruelty, all of the blood and the stretching of the body are now over, and the Son of God who became flesh has now paid the debt in full. He has become the world's Redeemer making full atonement for all our sins. He will become the Saviour of anyone who accepts him as Lord and Saviour. Thank God for this sublime picture of the Suffering Servant in his deepest agony.

QUESTIONS

Chapter I

1. Characterize briefly God's ideal man.
2. Which psalm gives you the best picture of him?
3. What part does God's Word play in building his character?
4. What qualities make up the ideal worshiper?
5. How can we measure up to such high demands today?

Chapter II

1. What is your favorite psalm of thanksgiving?
2. Name the gifts from God the poet mentions in Psalm 103: 1–5.
3. How is God pictured in Psalm 103: 8–14?
4. From what psalm do we get the "Doxology"?
5. In Psalm 116 what does the psalmist promise God?

Chapter III

1. Memorize and quote Psalm 23.
2. Who is the author of Psalm 23?
3. Name the blessings the author receives from the Shepherd.
4. What did the poet mean by: "He restoreth my soul"?
5. How did Jesus use and apply this psalm? (John 10.)

Chapter IV

1. How much of our Bible did the psalmists have?
2. What does the word "Torah" or "law" mean in the Psalms?
3. In what psalms do you find the best references to God's Word?
4. List the four references in Psalm 119 that mean most to you.
5. How will the study of this chapter affect your behavior?

Chapter V

1. How did David deal with his sin? (Psalm 51.)
2. How much blame did he take upon himself?
3. Why did he want a new heart?
4. How could he hope to have music in his soul again?
5. What is the first impulse of a saved soul? (Psalm 51: 13.)

Chapter VI

1. How did David deal with his sin before Nathan came to him? (Psalm 32: 3–4)
2. What are the three aspects of sin mentioned in Psalm 32?

3. List the three aspects of forgiveness as God works.
4. Sum up the points in David's experience (Psalm 40: 1–3).
5. What would you tell a sinner about the way to salvation?

Chapter VII

1. What is the psalmist's recipe for peace and serenity?
2. What picture is before you in Psalm 34: 7?
3. List the five verbs that stand out prominently in Psalm 37: 3–7.
4. Memorize and quote Psalm 40: 17.
5. What assurance is recorded in Psalm 73: 23–25?

Chapter VIII

1. Why did the people want to go to the sanctuary?
2. How could we help others as we travel? (Psalm 84: 6.)
3. What is the picture in Psalm 42: 1-4?
4. In Psalm 73 what was the psalmist's problem?
5. How and where did he find the solution?

Chapter IX

1. Name the psalms that are most specifically messianic.
2. Who is the King pictured in Psalm 2?
3. Describe the King's army pictured in Psalm 110?
4. State the specific fulfilments of Psalm 22 in the New Testament.
5. How will your life be changed by this study?